Own Your Journey

Daily Lessons in Self-Leadership

By:

Stacy Wood

And into the forest I go, to lose my mind and find my soul.

-John Muir

Background:

In her first book, Journey Through the Woods, author & executive coach Stacy Wood provided a framework for readers to clarify their goals, dreams, and intentions in life.

Stacy returns with her second book, *Own Your Journey*, to help the curious, the dreamers, the learners, and the explorers of life to take control of their future by

Owning Your Journey!

The path to a fulfilling life is paved by intentional self-leadership.

The book is designed with bite-sized daily learnings that are easily digestible, so that you can remain focused and on track as you intentionally pursue living the life you desire.

You can learn more about Stacy and her work at www.ttwoods.com

Introduction:

Life doesn't come with a road map.

We often start out on a trail of our best intentions only to be pulled or swayed onto other paths that intersect with our own.

In a world that constantly presents us with shiny new things, Insta-Celebrity, having it all, and overnight success, it is easy to feel as though we aren't enough, don't measure up, or will never find our way. It is easy to lose sight of our own journey, and instead we begin to live vicariously through the journey of others. We lose our connection to self by continuously looking externally for validation, approval, inspiration, and entertainment.

ENOUGH.

You deserve better!

You deserve to live a life full of intention. And that begins today!

You have the power to cultivate a life you love, but it does require you to revive your self-leadership skills. In this book you will be encouraged to expand your awareness, connect deeper with yourself, learn to vibrate at a higher frequency, cultivate your confidence, and clearly identify what matters to you. As these pieces come together, you will be sharpening the saw of self-leadership.

I have combined various lessons taught throughout history, the science that supports our ability to thrive, stories of my own journey as well as that of former clients (all names have been changed to protect their anonymity), and the wisdom of top thought leaders to holistically support your Own Journey.

~

As a mother, wife, daughter, and business owner, I know the stress of being pulled in 50 directions. Everyone wants a piece of your time. If you are reading this book, you are likely a high achiever, and in addition to being the best version of yourself I'm willing to bet that you often want to help those around you.

This is not a bad thing! However, the challenge is that as a society we have set unrealistic expectations stating that we can do it all, all at once.

What we really need is to filter out the fluff and noise; We need to get back to basics. To become good leaders of self we must maintain clarity around what matters, give attention to that which we are pursuing, and stay fiercely focused on those ideas and passions.

Simple in concept, yes; But very challenging in application.

You are not alone; you are not broken.

You are simply human.

~

I work with hundreds of women and men from around the globe who are productive and successful people; yet they *still* struggle to keep their eye on the ball and to stay committed to their personal journey in life.

Our nature as a leader of family, team, friends, or organization is to put our own needs last. But by doing so, we hinder our ability to grow in authenticity and therefore limit our capacity to lead others. To find our authentic path, we must balance our own needs with those of others.

In this book, I will give you easy to digest concepts each day so that you are able to maintain focus and remain on track for your Own Journey.

To begin, simply start on Week 1/Day 1. You need not wait for January 1st! Jump right in today and get started.

I highly recommend that you download the accompanying *Reader's Journal* template for free on my website, https://www.ttwoods.com/own-your-journey. Use this daily to take notes, and record your reactions, your inspirations, your struggles, and your personal action plan.

~

This book can be read year after year to refresh your skills of self-leadership as you strive towards Owning Your Journey. When you enter a season of change and find you are seeking/accepting/being forced to pivot, this book will once again be a lifeline that helps you to redirect your energy and thoughts in the proper direction.

I love writing in books (don't tell the librarians!) and make many notes to myself in every book that I own. I encourage you to do the same; make notes in the margins or mark especially powerful passages for yourself. This should serve as a personal guidebook to motivate, challenge, and encourage you.

~

You will find that I often refer to the Universe, Energy, and Nature in the book. For me, the Universe is an energy field that is the supreme supplier of all in this world. I believe the Universe wants to help us if we are open to it. Energy is carried by each of us. When we are carrying negative energy or are not aligned in our energy and actions, we struggle to find footing on our path. Many references will draw your attention to your personal energy so that you become aware of its power and importance along your Journey. Nature is the realm of life and drives the energy patterns within all life. Nature teaches us about patterns, balance, and growth. We will explore Nature's lessons and look to it as a resource for personal grounding and growth throughout the book.

We each live our own spiritual path; for you this may be interpreted as God or another higher power. You may not believe in a spiritual realm, but deeply in the scientific realm. Or you may fall somewhere in between.

Take the guidance from these passages and apply it through the lens of your *own* beliefs and spiritual path. This book is not meant to persuade, inhibit, or otherwise influence your spiritual beliefs. I encourage you to live in YOUR truth; and if you are seeking to *find* your spiritual truth, maybe these reflections will inspire you.

~

It is worth noting that I am an imperfect human who does not pretend to be a master of all things that impact my Own Journey. Personally, I have moments when I overreact, I lean into fear, I doubt myself, I get lazy, I fail to be as grateful, giving, or positive as I should be. Yet I am seeking to grow-as-I-go by being a student of life, of scholars, of nature, and of wise humans who have come before me.

Reading this book does not mean you will magically be a master of your journey. However, it *will* help to steer you on the right course, and it will help you to be more self-aware when you are off track. Pursuing your Own Journey will be a daily practice for the rest of your life; it is not a destination of perfection, but rather a way of living.

My hope is that this book will serve as a reminder for you, as it does for me, that each day is a new opportunity. Each new day is a chance to start fresh, to keep trying, to make progress in our growth as we work towards the owning our journey!

~

Who is this book for?

It is for you.

This book is for anyone who sees the value in empowering themselves to be the best they can, to achieve their goals, and to build joy into their lives.

I originally began this book writing to the traditionally employed people of the USA. I want to inspire each person to take charge of their future and their destiny; to empower themselves to speak up, set goals, make a plan, and work towards their True North.   To inspire individuals to take ownership of their journey, and to stop waiting for permission or approval.

But as it turns out, I have written this book for everyone: the Corporate Types, Stay at Home Parents, Business Owners, Dreamers, Students, Grandparents, Teachers, Volunteers, and anyone else. For those who are already slaying it on their journey, AND for those who are struggling at this moment.

This book provides universal truths for every human.

We all begin at different places on our journey, but the lessons are for each of us.

~

How to read this book:

Begin with Week 1, Day 1 (you may select any day of the week as Day 1; we recommend Sunday for easy pacing … but there are no rules). From there, simply follow the cadence of the book. You will have inspirational learning messages on Days 1 – 6 each week. Day 7 is a space to pause, and to allow for intention setting as you reflect upon what you absorbed that week.

If you get off track, don't waste energy worrying about it. Simply pick up where you left off as soon as possible. One of the principles of Self-Leadership is consistency, and I encourage you to practice that daily by committing to this process.

You will find that each day has 2 parts: *Get Inspired* and *Get Aligned*. You will then find a blank page on Day 7 of each week; this is a reflective space for you to *Make a Ripple*.

Please use them as follows …

Get Inspired:

This passage will provide you with inspiration and may challenge your current views and / or habits. These snippets are taken from philosophy, thought leaders, science, and other inspirational interviews or quotes. I invite you to take the time to deeply digest each passage as you consider its meaning in your world.

Considering different advice on age-old topics can provide the inspiration needed for change or commitment in your life.

Get Aligned:

This section will help you apply the *Inspirational Passage* into action for yourself as you pursue next-level personal leadership. This is where you reflect on your daily life; Consider how the wisdom from the inspirational passage applies specifically to your daily living. Moving from abstract concepts to concrete observations will strengthen their application in your life.

When you are willing to invoke personal awareness, you will find deeper growth!

Make a Ripple:

The seventh day of each week is reserved for your reflections. There are no lessons or passages to consider; this space was designed to encourage your ability to implement change, by allowing space for you to make personal notes to yourself.

What resonates with you? How will you apply that concept to your journey?

Go ahead, grab a pen and make it personal … make a ripple in your pond of status quo and see what bubbles up!

~

BEGIN

In this moment, I challenge you:

What will you do with this one precious life of yours?

Will you aimlessly follow other peoples' paths, or will you be brave enough to carve your own path and Own Your Journey along the way?

We are all in pursuit of a journey that is uniquely ours; do not be afraid of your path, instead rise to meet it and enjoy the journey!

The path to a fulfilling life is paved by intentional self-leadership.

Wishing you an amazing journey,

~Stacy

Dedicated to my beautiful children …

Your presence makes me work to be a better person every day. My wish is to support and inspire both of you to Own Your Journey throughout life!

~ xoxo ~

PART 1:

Have Awareness; Know Your Vision

"If I paint a wild horse, you might not see the horse... but surely you will see the wildness!"
— Pablo Picasso

PART 2:

Align Your Mindset

"You must learn a new way to think before you can master a new way to be."

-Marianne Williamson

PART 3:

Cultivate Your Presence

"Maybe you are searching among the branches for what only appears in the roots."

– Maulana Rumi

PART 4:

Commit to Action

"If there's a book that you want to read, but it hasn't been written yet, then you must write it."
— Toni Morrison

THE MODEL OF

SELF-LEADERSHIP

SEE THE VISION

Let the Fire in your belly ignite! See the Vision.

ALIGN YOUR MINDSET

Breathe life into your vision by aligning a productive mindset.

CULTIVATE YOUR PRESENCE

Grow in your presence and ability to show up for yourself.

EXECUTE THOUGHTFUL ACTION

Benefit from the cumulative ripple effect of repetition.

PART 1:

Have Awareness;
Know Your Vision

"If I paint a wild horse, you might not see the horse... but surely you will see the wildness!"
— *Pablo Picasso*

Week 1, Day 1

<u>Get Inspired:</u>

Vision is defined by *Oxford Languages* as:

"The ability to think about or plan the future with imagination or wisdom."

<u>Get Aligned:</u>

If I could sprinkle pixie dust on these pages, THIS would be the moment! I invite you to read that definition of Vision again, and this time imagine glitter and pixie dust floating around you as you do.

This definition of vision is so freeing, so light, and so encouraging. THIS is what I refer to when I talk about your vision. There is no pressure attached to your imagination of the future or the wisdom that is held deep inside of you. It just flows freely when it is ready, and when we are still enough to listen to it.

For many of us, we have been programmed for years to let go of our ability to conjure up our visions. We have been taught to stay in the moment, to plan logistically for the future of tasks that are demanded of us, and to be productive.

But if you speak to an artist, you will find that finding your vision isn't a process we can demand or dictate with logic. An artist will tell you that their ideas/vision "just come to them". They have trained themselves to stay in an open-minded space that allows ideas to flow without being stifled.

The good news is that we were ALL born with this ability, and therefore it remains deep in our DNA. We can recall this skill and bring it forward in our lives again. There are 3 basic ways to train our brains to invite the vision:

First, embrace the Mind Map or Brainstorm. Grab a blank piece of paper (even better, grab a poster board or big white board), and write down every idea that you have as it comes to you. The only rules are that you cannot filter ideas. If you think it, you must write it. Once you are out of thoughts, go back and make sense of the pile; group your brain dump into categories so that you can see your thought patterns emerging.

Second, allow yourself to Daydream. The next time you are waiting in line, riding an elevator, or stuck in traffic … don't reach for your phone. Instead, turn off the music, put your phone away, and just be. Let your mind wander and see where it goes! You might be surprised at the crazy twists and turns that it generates when given free rein.

And finally, embrace Doodling. Give yourself a blank sheet of paper and pens or pencils (bonus points if you have colored pens close by). When you are bored or stuck on a hard topic, just put pen to paper and see what happens. Another great time to do this is with your kids. Give everyone paper and markers or crayons, and just draw. There are no restrictions, no directions, just freedom. You will find this exercise is typically very easy for young children, but difficult for us. Keep practicing, it gets easier with time and really starts to open your brain's thoughts!

Week 1, Day 2

<u>Get Inspired:</u>

The concept of *'self-leadership'* was first introduced in organizational management literature by Charles C. Manz (1983).

He later defined it as a "comprehensive self-influence perspective that concerns leading oneself toward performance of naturally motivating tasks as well as managing oneself to do work that must be done but is not naturally motivating."

-Charles C. Manz, 1986

<u>Get Aligned:</u>

Self-Leadership is a fairly new concept considering that it was only introduced in the late 1900's. This means that we have not had much exposure to the concept and are still learning to understand it well.

According to Manz, it requires two efforts:

1- Influencing ourselves to embrace tasks that naturally motivate us (embracing the things we enjoy doing).
2- Self-management to ensure we are doing the work we find important but tend to dislike.

Striking a balance between that which we love and that which we ought to do is easy on paper, but difficult in real life. Pause to consider which side of the coin you find yourself leaning towards in difficult times. Do you punish yourself with only the "must-do" items, or do you hide in the tasks that you enjoy the most?

Each day is a new opportunity to find that balance and strive to exhibit a good model of self-leadership.

Week 1, Day 3

Get Inspired:

"Life isn't about finding yourself. Life is about creating yourself."
— George Bernard Shaw

Get Aligned:

This quote by Shaw is possibly one of the most powerful concepts for us to embrace.

We can spend a lifetime trying to "find" ourselves … but that implies that we have been lost our entire lives!

Instead, take the time to create the person that you want to be. You can BE any type of person that you imagine.

Take the time to be introspective and honest with yourself. Don't be afraid to dream and envision the person you want to be/ the life you want to live. Owning Your Journey means that YOU are the author of your personal manuscript.

Week 1, Day 4

Get Inspired:

Humans are puzzle solvers. Our drive to uncover mysteries, solve puzzles, and work through problems is a huge piece of what has made us the species that we are today. Curiosity is essential to our DNA.

Get Aligned:

If you continue to deaden your brain with mindless scrolling through apps, flipping TV channels, or otherwise numbing yourself, you are deadening your drive to be a puzzle solver. Instead, create an actual puzzle to jumpstart your brain. Work a jigsaw puzzle, visit an escape room, go on a scavenger hunt, read a mystery novel. Each task has its own unique way of tapping into those super-powers that make you human! Inspire others by inviting them to join you in such activities. Reignite your team at work by creating a puzzle solving atmosphere on a regular basis through both brainstorming sessions and team building events.

Weel 1, Day 5

Get Inspired:

"Take time to marvel at the wonders of life."

-G.W.F.

Get Aligned:

The Universe has cooked up some spectacular wonders to behold. Seek them out, travel the world, explore your town, visit your state parks.

Disconnect from your routine on occasion and push yourself to create an adventure in a new space. Your soul will be delighted with surprises.

What would you like to visit or experience in this lifetime? Create a bucket-list for your family and hang it for inspiration when making plans.

~

Building your vision as part of Owning Your Journey doesn't only apply to our work and education. It applies to all of the spaces in our lives, both big and small. When you take note of the world around you, those inspirations can and will spill over into a variety of moments in your life.

Week 1, Day 6

Get Inspired:

"Do not be too timid and squeamish about your actions. All life is an experiment."

-Ralph Waldo Emerson

Get Aligned:

There is no guidebook or manual for how to live life properly. We have been gifted with unique and individual brains, and therefore individual dreams.

Grab your dreams, visualize them, and pursue them.

This is the great experiment, what will work and what will redirect your efforts?

To get started, keep a journal, and let all of your smallest to wildest dreams live safely there. Get comfortable with allowing yourself to visualize a path and future that resonates with your soul. Slowly, you will begin to trust your dreams and make some fruitful efforts to get there.

Spark curiosity in others by sharing your dreams and your adventures in pursuing those dreams. They may not always work out as planned, but you will always have interesting stories to share.

Week 1, Day 7

Reflect:

What inspired you this week?

What will you carry forward?

Week 2, Day 1

Get Inspired:

Be the designer of your world and not merely the consumer of it.

-James Clear

Get Aligned:

We all know those people, the ones who are takers. They take whatever help, attention, energy, and resources that they can from everyone around them. At first, we may find ourselves attracted to these takers because they are "interested" in us. After some time, however, we find these people exhausting to be around as we recognize their true intent, and slowly begin to limit our time with them.

You may not be a taker from *others*, but how do you show up for *yourself* in life? Have you ever stopped to consider if YOU are a taker from your OWN life?

Are you always desperately <u>consuming</u> the energy, joy, and possibilities from each situation … or are you looking to <u>design</u> energy, joy, and possibilities in every facet of your life?

There are boundless missed opportunities if you ride through life merely consuming that which presents itself to you.

As a leader of self on a quest to Own Your Journey, you should be looking for ways to design and build key high frequency elements into all areas of life: joy, hope, excitement, possibility, positive energy, puzzle solving, and so much more.

Week 2, Day 2

Get Inspired:

"Won't you be walking in your predecessors' footsteps? I surely will use the older path, but if I had a shorter and smoother way, I'll blaze a trail there. The ones who pioneered these paths aren't our masters, but our guides. Truth stands open to everyone, it has been monopolized."

-Seneca,

Moral Letters, 33.11

Get Aligned:

Such strong words for a world where we may feel conflicted about charting our own course verses following in a great predecessors' footsteps.

We should learn from those before us who have gained great amounts of knowledge. But never be complacent to think this is the only path forward. Innovation comes from finding new ways forward.

Strike that balance between respectful learning from other leaders, combined with being strong enough to cut your own path when you feel a calling towards it. Be brave enough to question what you know and to embrace a vision for Your Journey that is as unique as you are.

Week 2, Day 3

Get Inspired:

'With the power of the soul, anything is possible."

-Jimi Hendrix

Get Aligned:

Reclaim the light within your soul.

Pause to realize what brings you joy in life? What sparks your creativity? We all had it once as a child, but often let it go as we turn into responsible adults.

We are not meant to go through life without excitement and joy. We are creatures of great capacity to love, learn, and experience exciting emotions.

Recall your hobbies of days past. Plan now to reconnect with an old hobby, or to try out a new potential hobby. Do not delay.

Sparking the light within you is the first step to finding and owning your unique vision for your life.

Week 2, Day 4

<u>Get Inspired:</u>

"Don't forget to ask: '*Is this the life I really want*'? Every time you get upset, a little bit of life leaves the body. Are these the things on which you want to spend that priceless resource? Don't be afraid to make a change, a big one."

-**Ryan Holiday**, *The Daily Stoic*, Portfolio/Penguin, 2016, pg. 52

<u>Get Aligned:</u>

Change can be scary. We have no guarantee of the outcome, and for the most part we are biologically designed to resist change.

However, to Holiday's point, you are whittling away at your one precious life if you are willing to live in mediocre versus making changes to work towards your ideal life. Ask yourself if you are unhappy with any portion of your life, and then brainstorm what type of life you truly desire. Begin to list the small (or big) actions you can take to live in harmony with your dreams. If your ideal life involves a need to move, begin by saving money intentionally and solely for that purpose. Investing in our dreams often involves sacrifice, but those will be well worth it if we are truly aligned with what our vision of a fulfilling life is.

Within your team or your family, have an open discussion about how you want to operate or live on a daily basis. Give everyone a chance to speak and share their thoughts. This cannot be a rushed conversation; it is likely one that will span a few hours or happen over a few weeks.

Align the feedback and look for common threads. From there, look for ways to collectively commit to supporting those common themes. Be clear with your family/team about the why, vision, goals, and process to get there.

Week 2, Day 5

Get Inspired:

"May your trails be crooked, winding, lonesome, and dangerous, leading to the most amazing view."

-Edward Abbey

Get Aligned:

Life is rarely simple and easy. We gain incredible opportunities for growth and perspective when we navigate the forests of difficulty, surprise, and uncertainty. Challenge yourself in the difficult times to look for the lessons you may learn or pause to reflect on the benefits gained after pushing through such hard times. Remember, the hardest climbs often lead to the most beautiful views.

Are you going through a hard time? Take a hike that ends with a spectacular view as a reminder that good things lay ahead.

Continue to ask yourself in the challenging times, where do I want to go, how do I want to live, and what lessons and I learning *right now* that may support my path on my Journey?

Week 2, Day 6

Get Inspired:

"Life is crazy; find your balance and enjoy the journey."

-Stacy Wood

Get Aligned:

Decades back, I decided that I needed a home-spun quote to inspire and motivate me every day. Above is the resulting passage that I still rely on to this day.

I challenge you to write a phrase or quote that encompasses how you want to show up in this world, and then post it in a place where you will see it every day!

Be brave enough to include your personal quote in the signature of your email; this will share your voice in a non-invasive way with others ... and might even inspire them to do the same.

Week 2, Day 7

Reflect:

What inspired you this week?

What will you carry forward?

Week 3, Day 1

Get Inspired:

"Human beings have an innate inner drive to be autonomous, self-determined, and connected to one another."

-Daniel Pink, (2011), *Drive,* Canongate Books., pg. 71

Get Aligned:

Feeling as though we belong is crucial to our make-up. But so is the need to be autonomous. We must be able to feel a sense of self-direction to be fully engaged and productive in all areas of our lives. When we flow in circles of people who experience autonomy and trust, they are more deeply bonded to one another.

Feed your need for autonomy. If you are working for a company/boss who micro-manages you too deeply, consider making a change that allows you more autonomy. Ask about a transfer, have an open conversation about their style, or choose to find a new job.

If you are in a relationship with a controlling partner, make a change. Get couples counseling or leave the relationship. (There are agencies that can help you with dangerous situations; do not wait!)

If you are a parent who exerts a high level of control over your children and rarely allows any autonomy, make a change. Consider ways in which you can extend autonomy safely and age appropriately to your child. For example, allow them to help you decide which vegetable you will serve with dinner.

~

A marker of self-leadership is the ability to be aware of how you are functioning on a daily basis … and to make changes if needed.

Week 3, Day 2

<u>Get Inspired:</u>

"Not all those who wander are lost."

-J.R.R. Tolkien

<u>Get Aligned:</u>

Don't be afraid to explore. When we become complacent with the "comfortable" or the "familiar", that is when we lose our zest for life and the higher order gift that makes humans superior puzzle solvers.

Curiosity is our friend, don't turn your back on it.

Consider what you have done outside of your comfort zone lately. I challenge you to embrace three new things you will do or seek out over the next month. Allow your mind to wander, allow your body to wander, allow yourself to explore your world.

It is guaranteed to renew a sense of ahh and wonder.

Week 3, Day 3

Get Inspired:

"Leadership requires two things: A vision of the world that does not yet exist, and the ability to communicate it."

-Simon Sinek

Get Aligned:

As we seek to be leaders of self, we must fulfill these two requirements as explained by Simon Sinek.

Begin with a vision of the world you WANT to live in. How do you function, what do your days look like, who is around you, what do you do with your time, where do you go, what emotions do you carry, what experiences do you have. Build an incredible vision in your mind that you will spend your life pursuing. It can be grand, or it can be basic … it just needs to be YOUR vision. This will be your personal guiding light as you pursue your True North through self-leadership.

Second, begin practicing how you will communicate this vision. As a leader of self, revisit this vision often and with clarity so that your mindset and actions can wrap around it. You will also need to communicate portions of this vision to the outside world. This will help to set boundaries, learning when to say Yes and when to say No. Communicating your vision will begin to attract the right people to you, and to gently push away those who cannot get onboard with your vision. It will help you to find the support and guidance of others who believe in your personal vision and your quest to Own Your Journey.

To effectively Own Your Journey, you must be brave and direct in facing your unique vision.

Week 3, Day 4

Get Inspired:

"Dream as if you'll live forever. Live as if you'll die today."

– James Dean

Get Aligned:

Dreams are the life source of innovation and success. Not all of our dreams will work out as we envision them, however, when we give them a fighting chance by making plans to pursue our dreams, we often stumble across something wonderful!

Allow your mind to wander, without pressure or a need to rush. Let the ideas naturally flow, grow, shift, and pivot. Cling to those dreams that resonate with your soul.

Live as though tomorrow isn't promised. Don't procrastinate or ignore the things that are most important to you. When you identify a dream that matters, you must begin immediately. Take tiny steps ... but take the steps.

Week 3, Day 5

Get Inspired:

"Whatever the mind can conceive and believe, it can achieve."

– Napoleon Hill

Get Aligned:

A vivid belief is likely are best weapon in any battle.

From illness to physical challenges, from getting a promotion to opening your own business. Whatever you BELIEVE is what will be.

Begin by picturing the outcome you desire. If you can't visualize it, keep trying. Make adjustments if needed but keep going.

Once you have a clear picture of what you will achieve/experience you can get to work on believing it. Give yourself a list of reasons why it WILL come to fruition. If you struggle, begin taking steps or actions to support the hypothesis. Build this trust and belief deep within your mind and your soul.

Cling to the ideas, the concepts, and the behaviors that support your vision. In time, they will evolve if you truly believe. It is often said that the difference between an entrepreneur who makes it verses one who fails is merely time. The one who truly believes will give it time, will pivot and shift as needed on details, but will always stay the course for the big picture.

Week 3, Day 6

Get Inspired:

"La vie est belle."

-French saying, "Life is Beautiful."

Get Aligned:

Life truly IS beautiful. A million small miracles are happening before our eyes each day, and yet we miss most of them or simply take them for granted.

If you think about the exact science involved in having a sunrise or sunset each day, it is astonishing.

When you consider the biology of what takes place each time you eat a meal, or see a loved one's face, or pet your dog, it is incredible.

When we are caught in the chaos of bouncing from task to task, it is helpful to pause and recall that *La vie est belle.* Lean into the most "basic" of miracles in your daily life, for they are rarely basic. This will keep you grounded when things seem tough, and inspired when things are going smoothly.

Week 3, Day 7

Reflect:

What inspired you this week?

What will you carry forward?

Week 4, Day 1

Get Inspired:

"Everything you can imagine is real."
— **Pablo Picasso**

Get Aligned:

Picasso is no doubt a visionary. He was able to imagine and create incredible works of art that were always unique. He found his success by being true to his imagination.

By embracing your unique ideas and imagination, you have the power to create something entirely new, fresh, and powerful. Not everyone will love it or understand it; that is ok so long as it resonates with you.

The only limitation to what we can achieve are the limits we place on our imagination and vision.

Week 4, Day 2

Get Inspired:

"Imperfection is beauty, madness is genius, and it's better to be absolutely ridiculous than absolutely boring."

— Marilyn Monroe

Get Aligned:

Playing it safe may seem like a smart choice. It keeps us grounded, ensures we have a job, an income, a home. But is playing it safe breeding genuine passion and fulfilling your soul?

I am not suggesting that you go jumping off the deep end right away but do consider how you can infuse more genuine passion into your life. How can you embrace your imperfections as opposed to fighting them?

It's hard, the expectations to be perfect are intense. Let's be honest, we live in a time with extreme standards. A time where it is common for individuals to inject a bacterium that can cause *botulism* into their faces; This is standard care for many people beginning in their 30's in an effort to keep that "perfect face".

If you are serious about Owning Your Journey, then you need to do just that … own YOUR journey, not someone else's journey. Begin to let yourself embrace those imperfections, do something ridiculous and take a break from boring once in a while. Stay committed to your vision of greatness, not someone else's.

Week 4, Day 3

Get Inspired:

"Live life to the fullest. You have to color outside the lines once in a while if you want to make your life a masterpiece. Laugh some every day. Keep growing, keep dreaming, keep following your heart. The important thing is not to stop questioning."

– Albert Einstein

Get Aligned:

It has been said that curious mind never grows old. We are the sole keepers of our internal energy; we should seek to constantly challenge ourselves so that we grow and learn. If we are so afraid of "messing up", we will never find our true strengths.

Albert Einstein is often referred to as a genius, and that I do not dispute. But many people do not know of his countless failed ideas. What made him a genius was his passion for nurturing his visions and working with them to make the most of each. He was brave enough to explore his visions. If he had not pursued his passions and visions without fear of failure, we may not have ever heard of his name.

~

Be bold enough to allow yourself to dream. Then take those dreams and create an action plan to execute on the dream. Because a dream without a plan will always remain as a dream, never making it to reality.

Week 4, Day 4

Get Inspired:

"If you don't have a vision, you're going to be stuck in what you know. And the only thing you know is what you've already seen."

- Iyanla Vanzant

Get Aligned:

No one wants to live their life on a hamster wheel. No option for change, no different way of looking at things, or with no new challenges.

When we close down our walls to stay routed in what we know, to limit our growth potential, and to be steeped in comfort … we are willingly giving up the ability to consider a different route, to try new things, to learn and grow, to try and fail, and to have abundant experiences along the way.

Your vision for the future is your own. It can be anything that you dream up! Don't limit yourself because "it may not come true". Challenge yourself to think beyond your wildest dreams, and then start chipping away at it.

Consider those around you who never talk of future dreams or plans, they are so fixated on what they know that they will rarely take a risk to try something new. Maybe you are currently caught in this same pattern. News Flash: You don't have to row down the same river of life forever! You can decide to take the left fork in the river, to paddle over to the riverbank, to go whitewater rafting, or even to paddle upstream. Surround yourself with people who also embrace a growth mindset and encourage each other to consider how you plan to show up on the river of life.

Week 4, Day 5

Get Inspired:

Napoleon Bonaparte

Napoleon Bonaparte is often considered the Godfather of creating the concept of a Mission Statement. He would give a "mission statement" before battle to his leaders. The "mission statement" was the guiding force, setting a clear picture of what the objective was and the desired outcome.

Subsequently, and unique to his time, he would allow those leaders to pursue the mission with tactics that made sense to them in the moment as opposed to a strict battle plan which Bonaparte had decreed.

Get Aligned:

Evolving from this concept, the modern-day Mission Statement is a staple for most businesses. I would argue that individuals need them, too.

Do you have a Personal Mission Statement? A statement or phrase that encapsulates who you are, how you will live, what your intentions are for a given period, or a growth process.

When we begin with a Personal Mission Statement, we have a clear lens of what we are working towards. This helps to serve not only our moral compass, but also to keep us focused on that which matters most. It becomes easier to identify when we get off course or are not acting in ways that serve our stated objectives in living.

As the chief commander of yourself, you should indeed create a Personal Mission Statement to guide your daily adventures. Support that by allowing yourself to be nimble in your approach to managing a variety of situations that arise on your journey. You don't need to have hard and fast rules regarding each challenge that you may face in life; simply know the purpose of your overall mission.

Week 4, Day 6

Get Inspired:

"It is not where you start out in life that counts the most, it is how you choose to face it."

-Angelina Jolie

Get Aligned:

Being a good leader does not mean you are the boss, it doesn't mean you have almighty power, or that you have all the answers.

It does mean that you recognize your role is to help lift others up, and to empower others to be their best and reach their goals.

When it comes to being a leader of self, the same applies. Empower yourself to dream big and achieve your goals. Inspire yourself to live in a way that aligns with your soul. Encourage yourself to try, even when it is hard. Support yourself with positive mantras, not negative talk. Commit to yourself through micro habits that will be the building blocks of success.

Believe in your unique vision of how you want to live and lead in this world. This will allow you to be secure as a leader of self so that you may in turn empower others to do the same.

Week 4, Day 7

<u>Reflect:</u>

What inspired you this week?

What will you carry forward?

Week 5, Day 1

<u>Get Inspired:</u>

"The future belongs to those who see possibilities before they become obvious."

-John Sculley

<u>Get Aligned:</u>

If you are waiting for "The Big Vision" to show up in your life and give you direction, you might want to think again. Sometimes we do have a BIG vision for the future, but more often than not, we make progress by keeping our eyes open to the smaller possibilities and opportunities that drift near us. Don't be afraid to look up from the beaten path and consider what could come next. Be willing to try new things, daydream about alternate paths, or journal about your goals.

If you are a new parent who is looking to create a childcare plan for your little one(s), be creative! Just because everyone you know goes to *The Fancy Daycare*, it may not be what works for you. Consider daycare, nannies, nanny-share, family, in-home care, alternate care plans, or any combination of the above that works for YOUR life and comfort level.

If you are working your way up the corporate ladder, you don't have to be a replica of everyone else within the firm. There are often zig-zag paths to the top, not just one straight line. Maintain respectful boundaries but be yourself, dress professionally but also in a manner that reflects your personality, jump outside of your comfort zone by talking to any and every person within the firm (both up and down the ladder), ask a potential mentor out to lunch, volunteer for the committee that interests you, and don't be afraid to express your career goals to your manager!

If we don't explore the boundaries, we may never see the alternate horizon or the hidden path that lies just ahead of us.

Week 5, Day 2

Get Inspired:

"Aging is not "lost youth" but a new stage of opportunity and strength."

– Betty Friedan

Get Aligned:

Time is a thief and time is a gift.

Both are true, and yet they are conflicting statements.

Time is a *thief* in the concept that it passes too quickly, and we cannot slow it down. Time is a *gift* because each moment we get with the people we love or doing the things we enjoy is indeed a gift, because tomorrow is not promised to us.

Our culture seems to be obsessed with slowing down aging. There are hundreds of injections, surgeries, creams, pills, and non-invasive treatments on the market, all aimed at reversing the signs of aging. Are we afraid of how we look, or are we afraid of how we feel? Are we afraid of the feeling that time is marching on, and we have yet to be living in our purpose?

My grandaddy used to say, "*The opposite of getting older is not a very good option*". He thought we earned our wrinkles, our slower pace, and our perspectives on life; and he was right! As much as I take his sentiment to heart, I am still human living in a culture obsessed with looking younger, and sometimes I, too, feel the pressure to "do more" about slow my aging process.

But what if what we are *really* afraid of is the FEELING that we get as we see ourselves age? The reminder in the mirror that we don't have unlimited time, and that feeling that we need to make our time on earth count.

That is something we can control! When we live in the model of self-leadership, we are maximizing our time and effort on this planet because we KNOW what we are living for, we are fully invested in our vision and our belief in our path, we are showing up in our truth, and we are committed to taking actionable baby steps toward those visions every single day.

That model allows us to live a life of purpose and fulfillment. That model allows us to not completely panic as we begin to age. That model teaches us that we have a choice to Own Our Journey and to make hard choices. And that model grounds us in our direction along our own unique path.

Week 5, Day 3

<u>Get Inspired:</u>

"Let us make our future now and let us make our dreams tomorrow's reality." – *Malala Yousafzai*

<u>Get Aligned:</u>

If you don't know Malala's name, you should. She is the young Pakistani woman who stands up for female education and human rights, she survived an assassination attempt by the Taliban in 2012 (she was only 15 years old), and she was the youngest person to receive the Nobel Peace Prize (in 2014) at the age of 17. Her book "I am Malala" was published in 2013.

If this woman cannot inspire you to take ownership of your visions and your dreams, I am not sure who can.

We may not all have a vision as bold and life changing as Malala's, but we each have a small spark somewhere inside of us. Does your spark reflect your career dreams, where you want to live, the type of family you want to build, a political / religious / humanitarian belief, a healthy way of life, your education, travel, creativity, or teaching? There are endless ideas that we can attach our thoughts to, but the ones that matter are the ones that develop deep in your soul.

Simple or complex, anything is possible. But nothing is possible if you don't first believe in it, and then create a plan to act in accordance with it.

Week 5, Day 4

Get Inspired:

"Optimism for me isn't a passive expectation that things will get better; it's a conviction that we can make things better."

-Melinda Gates

Get Aligned:

We are hard wired to be self-leaders. We each have dreams, visions, goals, and desires for how to live. We are designed to lean on ourselves, and to connect with others along the way. The model of self-leadership is coded within our DNA.

This means that we each have the power to reach in and begin.

Start listening to yourself; discover what your self-determined factors are, what your big ideas include, and who you really want within your inner circle.

If you are nervous or unsure of where to begin, starting with your vision is the first step. Keep listening to your dreams, your daydreams, and those nagging reoccurring thoughts. Go for a walk with no music and no phone; this is almost always a guarantee that an idea will show itself to you. Don't judge the size of your idea; it may be small or may be enormous. Give it space to grow and develop. Trust that your own thoughts won't let you down. As the idea takes shape over time, you will begin to feel an affinity towards it, and this is when you know you are on to something that was made just for you!

Week 5, Day 5

Get Inspired:

"Look beyond the present circumstances, imagine a brighter future."

-Lailah Gifty Akita

Get Aligned:

I have been urging you to listen to your heart, to find your vision, and to really grasp hold of it. But what exactly should you be looking for?

Your vision shouldn't be self-centered, harmful to others, petty, or otherwise shallow. Your big vision/s should be full of inspiration, passion, curiosity, and hopefulness. They should indicate your intent of how you will live in alignment with the tangible goal.

The easiest way to describe it is through example. These are not an all-inclusive list; think instead of them as mini models of what you may be inclined towards ... and then apply your own big thoughts and dreams.

Sample #1:

Don't focus on "I want to lose 10 pounds". That is a short-term self-centered goal.

Instead, focus your dream on something deeper such as "I intend to make healthy choices to support a balanced lifestyle and to invest in my long-term health".

Sample #2:

Don't focus on "I want to make $500,000 annually".

Instead, focus your dream to be something more abundant in all areas, for example, "I plan to thrive in all ways at work which will provide me with unlimited financial potential so that I can support my family, my community, and my planet. I want to earn more than enough money to live comfortably, to invest in others, and to have the ability to experience life in a way that ignites my soul".

Sample #3:

Don't focus on "I want to have 3 children by the time I am 38".

Instead, approach it from the space of "I intend to raise a healthy and happy family, to provide love and comfort to 3 amazing children, and to do so while I still feel young and vibrant enough to remain engaged and interactive".

~

What is your personal calling to be the best version of yourself?

Week 5, Day 6

Get Inspired:

"Getting in touch with your true self must be your first priority."

-Tom Hopkins

Get Aligned:

Knowing yourself is the only place to begin.

If you don't know your true self, how will you know where you want to go, what you want to achieve, or what your personal moral compass is?

The easiest way to know yourself is to have a conversation. Dig deep with yourself and ask some key questions:

What are your big dreams?

What is your moral compass?

How do you want to live this life?

What motivates you?

How do you self-sabotage?

Follow each with a series of "Why" questions to get to the root of your true self. Strive for a series of 5 "Why Questions" as you peel back the layers of the onion on each topic.

This will not be done in a day; this is a life-long skill that we must repeat often to stay connected with ourselves.

Week 5, Day 7

Reflect:

What inspired you this week?

What will you carry forward?

Week 6, Day 1

Get Inspired:

"To love ourselves and support each other in the process of becoming real is perhaps the greatest single act of daring greatly."

Brené Brown. (2012). *"Daring Greatly: How the Courage to Be Vulnerable Transforms the Way We Live, Love, Parent, and Lead"*, Penguin. p.96.

Get Aligned:

Daring Greatly… the art of not giving a Fuck about what others think!

Daring greatly means you are showing up comfortable in your skin, your thoughts, and your direction. That you believe in your journey.

Will you be brave enough to support others on their unique journey of authenticity?

If you can do that, why would you not extend that same compassion and support to yourself?

When we give ourselves permission to visualize, believe in, and own our goals/dreams, we can begin to build a self-love around these concepts. It is not selfish to be working towards a personal goal or path in life. It only becomes selfish if you neglect or hurt others to reach your goals.

Maybe if we took the time to know and love ourselves, we wouldn't always be in search of public approval. We could rest comfortably in our strengths and in our efforts to grow and reach our stated goals. We could let go of the need to please everyone around us, or to live up to someone else's goals.

Begin by clearly knowing your True North, what matters most to you. From there, visit the concept often and reaffirm for yourself that there is purpose behind your choices and actions as you strive towards the larger goal of living in harmony with your True North.

Week 6, Day 2

Get Inspired:

"Most people are living in an illusion based on someone else's beliefs."

— Jen Sincero

Get Aligned:

Are you busy climbing someone else's ladder?

Or have you defined what matters to you and what you want to accomplish in this life?

We must each define our own True North: That path that speaks to our soul and fills our hearts; The process of defining the magical pursuit of a summit which calls uniquely to you.

Begin by blocking out the noise and allowing yourself to listen to your own thoughts. Brainstorm and Mind Map all your thoughts. Later, go back and edit the list down to the things that truly sing to you and feel as though you would actually follow through on pursuing. These are your anchors to your True North, to your pursuit of your own intentional life.

Week 6, Day 3

Get Inspired:

"The whole point of being alive is to evolve into the complete person you were intended to be."

– Oprah Winfrey

Get Aligned:

Growth often involves growing pains. It involves mistakes and lessons learned along the way. None of us learned to walk without falling in the process.

Be bold enough to let go of what everyone else thinks of you. Yes, it hurts when others disapprove of our choices or put us down; being told we aren't "good enough" stings.

But it is a place to start. A place from where we can improve. A place from where we can push ourselves to be more.

This growth process is the only way that we become who we were meant to be. Self-growth is synonymous with self-leadership. Be brave enough to envision who you want to be, and then embrace the growth process along the way.

Week 6, Day 4

Get Inspired:

In life, carry a blend of Ethos vs. Logos vs. Pathos.

Ethos is the ethical appeal or your credibility.

Logos is the logical appeal or your strength of argument or rational thought.

Pathos is the emotional appeal or the passion you exhibit.

Get Aligned:

To be a leader of self, you must know yourself. Know your moral code and live by it fiercely. If you have never done so, take time to write down what *Ethos* you live by.

When you begin to feel overly emotional or chaotic in your thoughts, take a moment to pause so that you can return to *Logos*. Use a pen and paper to keep your thoughts clear and focused when things get crazy in life; journaling has long been a key habit for many successful people to maintain their *Logos*.

And finally, embrace your *Pathos* or passion for life. Be careful to acknowledge that this can turn negative if not checked on occasion. Keep your passion high with positive intent. Of note, when your passion transforms to anger, you are no longer living in *Pathos*.

Week 6, Day 5

Get Inspired:

Know your *Telos.*

Telos is a term used often by Aristotle which refers to the end purpose or goal of a person or their life.

Get Aligned:

Dig deeper into who you are. Build awareness of self through your *Telos.*

~

Why are you here?

What mark will you leave on this planet?

Can you do good each day?

What is your role in life?

~

All of these questions support the development of your *Telos.* This is not a 10minute exercise. This is a life-long pursuit.

Lean into the concept of knowing what you are living for and design your life around that *Telos.*

Week 6, Day 6

Get Inspired:

"Boredom is only for boring people with no imagination."

-Tim Tharp

Get Aligned:

When we seek boredom, we create inner peace. It allows our heart rate and blood pressure to slow, our brain relaxes and is able to absorb new stimuli, creativity boosts, and our creative problem-solving skills improve.

Ditch your devices and instead create space for boredom.

Next time you are waiting in line, resist the urge to pull out your phone. Instead, simply look around and observe all that is in front of you.

Boredom opens our minds to our vision.

~

Model for your children what boredom looks like.

They may fuss now, but they will thank you when they are older.

Week 6, Day 7

<u>Reflect:</u>

What inspired you this week?

What will you carry forward?

Week 7, Day 1

Get Inspired:

"Do what you feel in your heart to be right for you will be criticized anyway. You will be damned if you do, and damned if you don't."

-Eleanor Roosevelt

Get Aligned:

When you finally tire of the game of trying to please the world around you, you can begin to get on with the art of living with intention.

This is a valiant step on the path to Owning Your Journey.

When pursuing your own beliefs, there is no need to be rude or disrespectful to others. Simply stand by your convictions and try to ignore the nay-sayers.

When I was planning to leave my lucrative and stable job in medical sales to build my own consulting firm, I was told by several clients and friends that I was making a bad choice, it was too risky, I was a fool not to take a safer path. I quietly thanked them for their concern, and then went about proving them wrong.

Your personal vision is just that, personal. Treat it with respect and love. You will be amazed by what it can do for you.

Week 7, Day 2

Get Inspired:

"He who has a way to life can bear almost any how."

-Friedrich Nietzsche

Get Aligned:

We simply cannot control all of the bad things that will happen to us and around us in life. Tragedy and difficulty will find us all at some point.

However, when we are equipped with leading ourselves in a positive manner, we are able to bear the difficulties without falling apart. To do this, we must have the awareness to build a vision of how we want to live and function. Visualize what is possible for you, what is essential to you, connect to your True North, and know what success looks like in your eyes.

We then align our minds with abundance and positive intent. Mindset matters as it is a driving force that impacts our actions and our beliefs. We should live in gratitude and embrace an affirmational mantra. Be comfortable knowing that life happens in seasons, and we must develop patience knowing that everything cannot happen all at once.

As our vision and mindset align into a positive and curious space, we begin to show up with an authentic presence. We accept that we are in charge of leading ourselves and must take responsibility for how we carry ourselves. We take time to invest in our self-care and self-development, knowing that life is a process of learning and growing at all times.

And finally, we embrace micro habits that support our vision of self-leadership. We execute consistently, giving ourselves grace for not being perfect. We move from dreaming to reality with thoughtful actions and the willingness to take tiny steps on a regular basis.

When we arm ourselves with this formula for navigating through the journey of life, we are more capable of handling the challenges when they face us. But make no mistake, this formula is not applied overnight. It is a lifelong pursuit of self-leadership that is cyclical in nature and requires patient practice.

Week 7, Day 3

Get Inspired:

"There is only one success, to be able to spend your life in your own way."

– Christopher Morley

Get Aligned:

Knowing and living for your True North is the only way to truly be at peace with yourself.

This doesn't mean we must be selfish and ignorant of others' needs. It means we should know what matters most to us, what our moral compass is, and how to live a life in pursuit of that vision.

Begin to Own Your Journey by living in clarity of your True North.

Week 7, Day 4

Get Inspired:

"It is the ultimate luxury to combine passion and contribution. It's also a very clear path to happiness."

-Sheryl Sandberg

Get Aligned:

Passion is that deep fire we have for something. The drive that wakes us up in the morning, that energizes our spirit, and helps us to get through the tough times. Contribution is the process of helping someone or something greater than us.

When we align these two things within our quest for self-leadership, we will accelerate our growth, and our happiness. This is not something we can fake, or something that will make our lives perfect. Combining passion and contribution will be a sure sign that you are indeed on your own path and working towards your True North. Sandberg calls this a luxury, and maybe it is, but I believe we can experience this luxury if we are willing to plan for it.

To do this, we must have a clear vision of what we believe in, what we want to solve, how we want to live, and/or where we want to go in life. This vision can guide your career, your hobbies, your investments, and/or your free time. The beauty of being a great leader of self means that you are free from the false belief that your job *must* be your passion or your contribution to life.

Sometimes, a job is just a means to put forth good effort and receive fair compensation in return. Your paycheck is what allows you to pursue your passion and contributions in your own time. If you are one of the lucky ones who has figured out how to combine both into your career, that is marvelous! But it is not a carrot that we all need to be lunging for.

A preacher friend once shared a story with me from one of her counseling sessions for a parishioner (*and of course was respectful enough to keep his identity anonymous*). The congregation member was conflicted and seeking guidance because his career did not reflect his deep religious and moral beliefs. His job wasn't in conflict with his beliefs, but he felt guilty that his work wasn't directly related to supporting the church.

Pastor D shared with him that we should never be ashamed of putting in an honest day's work to put food on our table and a roof over our heads, and to provide for our family. That our work isn't the *only* way to serve our beliefs in life. We can take the money we earn or the flexible schedule that we acquire which allows us to use our time and our gifts to give back to our passions (in this case, his passion was the church and his mission work).

Do you know your passions and what contributions you want to make in life? Get started brainstorming on that today and look for small areas of time or space where you can apply these efforts!

Week 7, Day 5

Get Inspired:

"I'd rather be a failure at something I love than a success at something I hate."

-George Burns

Get Aligned:

As an executive coach, I work with many driven and high performing individuals. One group of professionals that I often work with are physicians. As we begin our work together, I always ask, "Why did you become a doctor?".

The top responses that I get are as follows:

1. "I love working with people and helping them."
2. "I was inspired by witnessing the illness of a family member/loved one growing up."
3. "I was good at science, and someone suggested I should be a physician."
4. "It was expected of me."

What I hear in these responses is:

1. I want to help others, and this seemed like an obvious way to do that.
2. I wanted to make a difference in the world.
3. I am smart, and so it appeared that I would excel in this field.
4. No one asked what passions I had, they wanted to ensure I had a finically sound future and a respectable job.

What I don't hear my clients say often is this:

1. I love the lifestyle.
2. I love the pressure of the job.
3. I love continuing to figure out the puzzle every day.
4. I love the personal challenge that comes within the profession.

And therefore, I am rarely surprised when I meet physicians' mid-career who are severely burned out. They are stressed to high levels, expected to be omnipresent, and continue to have their workload added to.

If only these folks had asked themselves long before med school what they love, and if they loved the physician lifestyle … maybe they would have chosen an alternate path or adjacent field of study. Maybe they would still become physicians, but not practice medicine in the same capacity as they have been doing for years.

Personally, I was on a straight path the Vet School for as long as I can remember. It was my passion, and I was determined to be an equine vet. I chose my undergraduate school based on this goal and earned my bachelor's degree in Equine & Animal Sciences. Luckily, when the time arrived to apply to Vet School, I had an awakening and realized that my passion for learning and caring for horses could always be a great hobby … but that I didn't want that career as a lifestyle. And so, my pivot began.

It is never too late to consider what we love, and to make that a bigger focus in our lives. When we lead with passion, we will find a different kind of success … a success that lives within our hearts and our souls (even if we never meet society's definition of success).

Week 7, Day 6

Get Inspired:

"It is nothing to die. It is frightful not to live."
— **Victor Hugo,** *Les Misérables*

Get Aligned:

Going through the motions of life without choosing to really live is a devastating way to exist.

You don't need extravagant budgets to truly embrace life. Get clear on what lights you up, what challenges you, and what feeds your curiosity. Lean into these spaces.

Those who are afraid to lose, afraid to try, afraid to look foolish are truly the ones who miss out on the chaotic and colorful pursuit of a life lived with passion.

We are all guaranteed death at some point. We don't know when it will come, and so we must seize each day with passion.

This doesn't mean you will always be happy, always be productive, or always be relaxed. It simply means that you are clear on what matters most in your life, and you aren't willing to ignore it.

You might work your entire life towards a goal that you never reach. But if this goal filled you with passion and the pursuit of it brought you joy, I'd argue that you truly lived and Owned Your Journey!

Week 7, Day 7

<u>Reflect:</u>

What inspired you this week?

What will you carry forward?

Week 8, Day 1

<u>Get Inspired:</u>

"The best remedy for those who are afraid, lonely or unhappy is to go outside, somewhere where they can be quite alone with the heavens, nature and God." – **Anne Frank**

<u>Get Aligned:</u>

Before we dive in, please note, if you are not religious or spiritual feel free to substitute your own words in this quote so that it resonates with your beliefs … but note that it should be SOMETHING that is more powerful than us humans (i.e., nature, the ocean, wind, etc.).

Anne Frank survived some of the most unimaginable life circumstances and did so as a child. The wisdom she shared in her diary is far beyond her years. Her concept of self-leadership is astonishing and developed at a young age out of a desperate need to survive.

The process of putting yourself in nature when times are difficult seems simple and trite, but the cumulative power of calmness, smallness, and opportunity that come with this interaction is always overwhelming. When we are reminded of how small we are in the Universe, how trivial some of our problems may be, and how much beauty is around us … it is hard not to have your spirits lifted.

Try this today:

Go outside and listen to how many different birdsongs you can hear.

Or,

If you aren't in an area that offers any wildlife, listen to a recording of the ocean, and feel the rhythm of the waves as they crash.

Be certain to take in the birds/ocean sounds. As your mind wanders, bring it back to active listening. After you find a few moments of stillness to listen to these sounds, take note of how you are feeling.

Are you more relaxed? More inquisitive? More open minded?

Being grounded in awareness will serve your ability to visualize your future.

Week 8, Day 2

Get Inspired:

"The first and best victory is to conquer self."

-Plato

Get Aligned:

Self, the most important of our relationships, and often the one most ignored.

If we refuse to know ourselves, how will we know where we want to go, how we want to live, and if we are on the right track?

When we refuse to really know ourselves, we find ourselves blaming others, living in a space of lack, and viewing the world from a pessimistic lens more often than we care to admit. This stems from the insecurity of an ambiguous identity.

Take the time to be with yourself, in your head, and in your heart. What lights you up, what gives you nerves, what makes you nauseous? Study how you react to various challenges, study how you react to joy, study how you react to those who are different than you. Getting to know Self will allow you to chart a course confidently knowing you are in pursuit of your True North.

Week 8, Day 3

Get Inspired:

"My mother told me to be a lady. And for her, that meant be your own person, be independent."

– Ruth Bader Ginsburg

Get Aligned:

There is no greater power than to truly be oneself. Sometimes showing up in your truth can be the scariest thing of all, but if we don't, we fail to truly live. You don't have to be a trend setter or boundary breaker, just keep showing up as yourself.

Your authenticity will attract the right people to you. Aligning with your truth will allow you to sleep at night. And being kind to your soul by acknowledging who you are as a person will pay you back in dividends.

Not everyone will get it, or support who you are and what you believe. That is ok, because you are the CEO of self. And you get to decide when and how to be authentically yourself.

Week 8, Day 4

<u>Get Inspired:</u>

"If you're always trying to be normal, you will never know how amazing you can be." – *Maya Angelou*

<u>Get Aligned:</u>

Jimi Hendrix, a Seattle native and African American legend (who is also believed to have been of Cherokee descent), is considered both one of the best artists and guitarists of all time. He was flashy, outspoken, and unique in his sound. Hendrix is known for turning the previously undesirable sound of guitar amplifier feedback into a mainstream effect. He also popularized fuzz distortion, stereophonic phasing effects, and countless other alterations with the guitar. The electrifying and unique approach he took to singing, guitar, and within his lyrics put him on the map.

Imagine if Hendrix had played it safe. Would we even know his name if he followed his predecessors, playing "traditional" guitar, and didn't express his individuality? An entire genre of music may not have been born.

As a mentor once shared with me, "Let your freak flag fly. People will either love it or hate it, but you will find your tribe!".

Week 8, Day 5

Get Inspired:

"Logic will get you from A to Z; imagination will get you everywhere."
— Albert Einstein

Get Aligned:

Logic and intelligence are very important factors when navigating life. But when we neglect to nurture our imagination and creativity, we shut out a huge vehicle to get us to the seemingly impossible places!

When we allow our brains to wander, to consider, and to imagine what could be … we open the door to achieving those ideas. If we cannot imagine it, we cannot visualize it. If we cannot visualize it, we will struggle to make it a reality.

This applies to your vision for work/productivity, your vision for relationships, your vision for helping others in life, and your vision of your health and happiness.

If you are in the habit of staying with your logical brain only, this will take practice. Make space each day for a few moments of doodling, brainstorming, or simple daydreaming. Don't stifle your ideas; just let them flow and see what floats up!

Week 8, Day 6

Get Inspired:

"Not how long, but how well you have lived is the main thing."

– Seneca

Get Aligned:

We often chase youth in our culture, while simultaneously chasing a long life.

What we are really after is the ability to experience life and live fully. What we crave is to find joy and peace, while remaining relevant.

These things are available to us, but not without potholes and disruptions along the way. The vibrant twists and turns combine to create a full story. That combination is the essence of truly living. Of not being afraid to step up and face what comes your way as you navigate your journey through life.

~

What makes for a life well-lived in YOUR book?

Take a moment to reflect on what matters: family, kindness, money, fame, health, travel, education. There are no right and wrong answers if you tap into your personal soul.

Week 8, Day 7

Reflect:

What inspired you this week?

What will you carry forward?

Week 9, Day 1

Get Inspired:

"To live is the rarest thing in the world. Most people just exist."

– Oscar Wilde

Get Aligned:

By experiencing life in a bigger way, we are truly living to the fullest. This might mean traveling, considering a new job, committing to a relationship, learning a new hobby, or simply seeing the state parks in your state.

When we choose to explore the world or the people around us, we open up an even deeper appreciation for what this life holds! There is so much that exists beyond our daily routines and comfortable spaces. Getting bogged down in the routine and responsibility of "getting through the day/week" leaves much to be desired.

I do not wish to live only to "make it through my to-do list". I want to soak in as much life as possible!

How do we do this?

By intentionally planning to make space for the things we love, the things that we are curious about, and the things that we don't yet know about.

Build an awareness of your passions, curiosities, and priorities. Keep these as a central focus and you will be

building an intentionally joyful life with every choice you
make.

Week 9, Day 2

Get Inspired:

"Success is loving life and daring to live it."

-Maya Angelou

Get Aligned:

So much of our world is focused on achieving "success". But what is that really?

Success is the ability to know what matters to you, and to pursue it. Success is knowing and living your values. Success is choosing joy, without apology. Success is being grateful for all that you have. Success is living in the now, not the past or the 'what may come'.

Stop chasing someone else's version of success. Stop chasing a social media fueled illusion of success. Stop chasing your yesterday's dream, and instead start focusing on today's.

Owning Your Journey does not mean you will meet society's measure of success, but it does prepare you to live a fulfilling life and to find joy along the way. Bonus- applying the concepts and principles of self-leadership will help you to achieve your goals, whether financial, title, relationship, health, or hobby related.

Week 9, Day 3

Get Inspired:

"Conscience is the voice of the soul."

-Polish Proverb

Get Aligned:

Your conscience, also referred to as your "gut feeling" is more powerful than you give it credit for! We are wired to have those connected feelings, yet we often train our brains to tune out the messages that lurk within.

I encourage you to begin listening to your gut, to your conscience, to your intuition. We can and SHOULD listen to those nudges of "something isn't quite right", or the ones that say "wow, this is amazing".

I find that as humans we tend to swing in two opposite directions in an attempt to ignore our conscience. We will either ignore the warning signs of trouble ahead in favor of "just moving forward", or conversely refuse to acknowledge our joy by ignoring the signals when things are clicking. The second is especially sad; when we are in a state of bliss or happiness and find ways to disrupt it because we are only comfortable with an agitated conscience. This default makes us truly our own worst enemy.

Practice listening to your gut. Just listen; you don't have to react. Take time to get comfortable with being aware of your inner state and pay attention to what comes in the future.

Soon you will slowly begin to trust this primitive but reliable inner gut.

Week 9, Day 4

Get Inspired:

"Life isn't about finding yourself, it's about creating yourself."

-George Bernard Shaw

Get Aligned:

Maybe you believe in destiny, and maybe you don't. That is irrelevant.

What matters is that you understand YOU are in the driver's seat of your life. When you decide to take ownership and create the person you aspire to be, you will find a new level of love and humbled appreciation for your abilities.

Don't wander aimlessly wondering who you are supposed to be. Decide how you want to live, how you want to show up in life, and begin the process of honestly pursuing that in action, thought, and reaction.

To be a leader of self on Your Own Journey, be clear in your awareness of who you are.

~

How do we convince others to create themselves? By simply asking and giving them the option. If you are a parent or a teacher or a leader, you have a divine responsibility to ASK those who follow you, "Who are you? Who do you want to be?".

Week 9, Day 5

Get Inspired:

"Find something you are passionate about and keep tremendously interested in it."

-Julia Child

Get Aligned:

Let's be honest, are you a "flavor of the week" type of person, or a "mint chocolate chip for life" type of person? When you consider your hobbies, have you made a life of trying new hobbies, or have you been committed to one or two?

(I'm a peanut-butter-chocolate ice cream for life, default to chardonnay, and all things horses type of girl ... but my wardrobe is constantly changing!)

I am often asked by clients if they are "bad" for falling into the category of always trying new things. The answer is absolutely not! For some people, the excitement of trying new things IS their hobby and is the process of finding joy in life. That adventurous spirit should not be squashed.

Conversely, if you are a stick-to-it kind of person, that is also valuable. You are the committed type who can usually work through tough times because you don't have to mentally battle yourself to stay committed.

However, when we stop to consider it, most of us have a combination of BOTH tendencies. Personally, I am the girl who orders the same meal at my favorite restaurants (every single time), I keep the same morning routine Monday –

Friday, and I have had the same passionate hobby since I was 10 years old (riding horses). However, when it comes to fashion and home décor, I love to change things up, often. When it comes to ideas for the business, I have a busy brain and so I let the new concepts flow, knowing that the 'right idea' will show up at some point. When it comes to travel, as a family we love to try new places with our children.

The trick is to recognize that we have BOTH the Stick-To-It mentality AND the Flow-With-It mentality inside of us... and to recognize when each is useful.

As you work on your self-leadership and Owning Your Journey, you will find and refine your vision. This is when it is time to align your mind around it and stay committed to nurturing it. Give it a fair chance before you pivot off to a new idea. It is normal to shift over time and as the seasons of life change; in these times we will generate new visions of how/when/where we want to pursue our journey.

Balancing that temptation to quickly shift when things get hard with a commitment to our ideas will be the litmus of your self-leadership. Allow yourself to go through the process: see the vision, align your mind around it, show up for it, and commit to actions that support it. Once you experience the full process and determine that the vision should be adjusted, go for it!

However, if you find that you are continuously avoiding the work to support your vision, then you are caught in a cycle of self-sabotage. Something must change if you want to make progress. It is time to consider if your vision is off, or if your commitment to it is off.

Week 9, Day 6

<u>Get Inspired:</u>

"What you do makes a difference, and you have to decide what kind of difference you want to make."

-Jane Goodall

<u>Get Aligned:</u>

Each of us has a mind that we can use for a good impact, or we can float through life without any thought to our moral compass or True North. The latter is a selfish and unsteady way to live.

You don't need to be in training to be the next Mother Theresa, but you should know that your choices impact others. We have a responsibility to balance our drive and ambition with our moral compass. We set an example for others with the choices we make.

If we have clarity on how we would like to positively impact the planet or the creatures on this planet, then we can make tiny choices each day that support that vision. We can indeed pursue our goals and ambitions while simultaneously putting good out into the world.

Week 9, Day 7

Reflect:

What inspired you this week?

What will you carry forward?

Week 10, Day 1

Get Inspired:

"To be yourself in a world that is constantly trying to make you something else is the greatest accomplishment."

— Ralph Waldo Emerson

Get Aligned:

You are unique. Cling to that uniqueness no matter what.

We live in a world that is constantly trying to convince us to be something else, to believe in a different dream, to have a different style, to work in a different way. The larger the presence of social media in our world, the more subconscious pressures we face. To resist those pressures, we must ask ourselves each day:

"Who am I?"

"What do I stand for?"

"What do I want to accomplish?"

"How do I intend to live?"

Own Your Journey by remaining aware of who you are, and who you want to be.

Week 10, Day 2

Get Inspired:

"If you don't stand for something you will fall for anything."

— Gordon A. Eadie

Get Aligned:

Our moral compass is our guide along our Journey of Life. This doesn't mean that we will always get it right, but it keeps us focused on where we *intend* to go and how we *intend* to live. It helps to keep the wolves at bay and the sun on our faces.

If we don't have a sense of our True North, we can easily be swayed to follow along anyone else's journey. We may become their pack-mule without realizing it.

Set up some guiderails for Your Own Journey by knowing what matters to you and keep it in focus at all times. This will help you to make a choice when you are at a crossroads, or when others are asking you to join them along their journey.

Week 10, Day 3

Get Inspired:

"Your goals are the road maps that guide you and show you what is possible for your life."

-Les Brown

Get Aligned:

There is indeed a heated debate on the topic of goals. Should we have them? Are they a waste of time, or do they inspire us?

Goals or not, we should at least have a vision in life of what we want to do and how we want to live / show up in this world. These visions will inspire us to take chances, to learn new skills, to try new things, or to double down on our current efforts. They guide us in what to say NO to, and what to say YES to. They are the puzzle that we are working to solve.

I have always been driven by my vision. My vision may have changed over the years, but I am true to what I see and how I want to live ... and I commit to a path to achieve that vision.

In high-school, I wanted to be an equine vet. And so, I took jobs and went to school to prepare for this vision.

At the end of my junior year of college, I had a realization that my vision had shifted. I no longer wanted my hobby to be my career. And so, I pivoted away from vet school and began planning for a different career.

After I was married, I had a strong vision for us to build and live on our own horse farm. We were young and didn't have much money, but we made it happen and created a beautiful little farm.

After we had children, I had overwhelming visions of being an entrepreneur. And so I began the long tedious path of researching, credentialling, building, opening, and growing my own business.

The vision CAN change. But if you never pause long enough to see the vision, how will you know if you are working towards your **own** goals?

Week 10, Day 4

<u>Get Inspired:</u>

"No longer chasing butterflies, Camila and I planted our garden so they could come to us."
— **Matthew McConaughey**, *Greenlights*

<u>Get Aligned:</u>

When you know what you want in life, you can plant the appropriate garden to attract those specific butterflies.

Don't spend your life chasing the shiny things, be clear on what matters to you and begin to build a world around that concept. It will take years, but the focused work will be worth it. *Of note, if Wanderlust is your THING, go for it! Your garden may be the garden of travel … the trick is to know what drives you.

Share your dreams. When you are crystal clear about what you are living for, people become curious, supportive, and generally want to help you achieve it.

Week 10, Day 5

<u>Get Inspired:</u>

"A healthy desire for wealth is not greed. It's a desire for life."

– Jen Sincero

<u>Get Aligned:</u>

Money is an uncomfortable topic to discuss with others, and often to even think about privately. We have a ton of emotional baggage tied up in our individual perceptions of what money stands for, our worthiness, and how to use it.

Begin by acknowledging that wanting to have a comfortable (or more indulgent) level of wealth to ensure financial stability in your life is not a sign of greediness. Ask the Universe to guide you in developing a plan and habits to build the wealth that will support your life.

*Of Note: Having resources <u>does</u> give you options in life of how to live, though be careful not to believe that it will provide happiness. Money is a means to provide a style of living, NOT a means to create happiness or joy.

~

As you ask the Universe to help guide you in building your wealth, be sure to believe and include a statement of HOW that wealth will pass <u>through</u> you to benefit others around you. From your family, to charities, to small businesses … your wealth enables you to invest in others, and that is a positive effect of wealth.

~

Visualizing what role money plays in your life is part of realizing your complete vision.

Week 10, Day 6

Get Inspired:

The 5 Levels of Leadership, by John Maxwell, teaches us that there are five consecutive levels of growth as a leader.

Level 1 — Position (no requirements to meet this entry level).

Level 2 — Permission (based on relationships, people follow because they choose to).

Level 3 — Production (leaders who produce results by inspiring followers to get things done).

Level 4 — People Development (leaders at this phase are recognizing and developing other leaders as often as possible).

Level 5 — Pinnacle (a lifelong pursuit of great self-leadership and development of other leaders can lead to this top level, which is hallmarked by your reputation).

Get Aligned:

These five levels of leadership are wonderful to understand and apply at the team level. But what impact do these levels have on your self-leadership journey, or do they even apply? I think they do.

Let's begin with Level 1 — Position. This is the assumption that we are all born with the basic ability to lead ourselves.

Moving on to Level 2 — Permission, this is the process of self-awareness to ensure that you truly know yourself.

Level 3 — Production involves committing to your goals and following through with the actions that support those goals.

As you improve your self-leadership, it naturally spills over to Level 4 — People Development; on the self-leadership model this would be the process of staying grounded in positive energy to inspire and support others along their unique journeys.

At the very top, Level 5 — Pinnacle, resonates directly as the lifelong pursuit of great self-leadership. We will never be perfect; we will always have some struggles in our self-leadership journey. But with daily attention and practice we can live at the Pinnacle level of continued growth.

As you work towards Owning Your Journey, consider where you are in the levels of self-leadership, and what you can do to move forward as we all strive for level 5.

Week 10, Day 7

Reflect:

What inspired you this week?

What will you carry forward?

Week 11, Day 1

Get Inspired:

"Listen to the wind, it talks. Listen to the silence, it speaks.
Listen to your heart, it knows."

-Native American Proverb

Get Aligned:

Awareness is the essence of a good self-leader.

When we train ourselves to notice the littlest things around us,
we are tapped into a deep level of awareness. This is the basic
building block for those who wish to be good leaders of self.

Start with Nature and with what you hear when sitting with
your own thoughts.

Take in what you see, hear, and feel. This is true awareness.
It can feel unsettling to sit in the quiet if you are accustomed
to a fast pace, but this will be some of the most therapeutic
times you have spent in a long time.

Week 11, Day 2

Get Inspired:

"Wanting to be someone else is a waste of the person you are."

-Kurt Cobain

Get Aligned:

The overwhelming message we receive in life is "Keep Up with Others". We even have a term for it, "Keeping Up with The Jones's".

This tunnel-like focus on fitting in, to keep up, to assimilate into achieving the same goals as everyone else, is dangerous. It pulls our attentions away from our True North, from the person we were meant to be.

Owning Your Journey requires you to fully acknowledge your personal goals and dreams in life, and to live authentically in alignment with them. This might mean running a separate race from your colleagues or spending your time and money differently than your friends.

It can be hard to be a wildflower in a field of roses, but it is so much more interesting!

Week 11, Day 3

Get Inspired:

"I can't imagine how anyone can say: 'I'm weak', and then remain so. After all, if you know it, why not fight against it, why not try to train your character?"

– Anne Frank

Get Aligned:

Sometimes we need the innocent views of children to remind us to get the hell out of our own way!

If you feel weak, what are you doing about it? Self-leadership demands that we see our weaknesses and do something to move us to a place of comfortable strength. This does not mean that you must go from weak to the best. It *does,* however, mean that once you identify something as a weakness you refuse to let it rule over you by instead training yourself to overcome, move past, or transform it.

Are you a procrastinator?

Do you get distracted by shiny object syndrome?

Do you cave to the opinions of others?

Do you refuse to hear the opinions of others?

Are you full of excuses as to why you can't achieve something?

Identify your weakness and begin to exercise the muscles around it so that you find peace with it. Train your brain as if you were training your body for fitness. You don't have to go from a couch-potato to becoming a Cross-Fit champion, but you should be able to walk a brisk mile without collapsing.

Decide what your goals are in addressing the weakness and then apply a few micro-habits that create supportive behaviors for these goals. Be aware of who you are, how you show up, and how you get in your own way!

Week 11, Day 4

Get Inspired:

"The life which is unexamined is not worth living."

-Plato

Get Aligned:

Spend time with yourself assessing what you love, what you dislike, and what you wish for your life.

If you do not take steps to create or cultivate this life, you risk leaving this world with disappointment. You may not reach all of your goals, but you will know that you have lived with intention and a clear heart, that you have done your best.

Make no apologies for your beliefs and your vision in life and be sure to make space for others to have their unique beliefs and opinions as well.

Week 11, Day 5

Get Inspired:

"Self-leadership is about awareness, tolerance, and not letting your own natural tendencies limit your potential."

-Scott Belsky

Get Aligned:

Awareness is the first step to improved self-leadership. As we take full notice of who we are, we can begin to examine how we want to live. From there we will cultivate a supportive mindset and presence for ourselves so that we can take actions to reach our big dreams and goals. None of these can move forward without self-awareness. Once you see your tendencies to get in your own way, do something about it. Get a coach, a therapist, a mentor, or an accountability partner. Do something to ensure that you won't hold yourself back from reaching your potential.

~

Inaction is merely a lazy excuse to stay stagnant.

Week 11, Day 6

Get Inspired:

"We don't inherit the Earth from our ancestors, we borrow it from our children."

-Native American Proverb

Get Aligned:

We may officially "own" a piece of land, meaning others cannot do with it what they will. But we never truly own the land. The earth is far more powerful than we are, and we have no claim to think we can manipulate its cycles or natural processes.

Owning Your Journey is not a process of taking the world by storm. Rather, it is a belief in yourself, a belief that you can carve your own path in life, and a commitment to do so without causing harm to those around you. Having the awareness to see your vision for life is important ... but should always be coupled with an awareness of the world around you. Be humbled by and derive your energy from the incredible natural resources around you.

Whatever mark we leave on this world, we are passing along to our children and their children.

Let it be a positive one.

Week 11, Day 7

<u>Reflect:</u>

What inspired you this week?

What will you carry forward?

Week 12, Day 1

Get Inspired:

To find your balance and to be grounded, we should bond with *physis* (nature or the natural order of the world).

-Epictetus, *Discourses*, 4.4.42

Get Aligned:

Epictetus (a well-known stoic) believed that we should strive to always keep ourselves in harmony with nature. This sentiment has been repeated by many scholars and successful people who have proceeded this book. If we are wise, we will listen to their collective wisdom.

Nature is an often quiet, but always powerful force. It can help us to remain centered, to learn about how our world operates, to reduce stress, and to restore our imaginations.

When is the last time that you rooted yourself on a patch of grass or sat on a rock, intentionally feeling the piece of earth that is beneath you?

I encourage you to try this exercise. It is incredibly powerful to be still and simply absorb the natural world. You will find that your mind opens, that your curiosity peaks, and that you feel more settled internally.

Grounding yourself in this manner brings you back to basic self-awareness and opens your mind to possibilities you may not have seen before.

Week 12, Day 2

<u>Get Inspired:</u>

A Lesson in Hormones

Men begin producing high levels of testosterone at the onset of puberty. Testosterone is linked to higher risk-taking tendencies, as well as feeling powerful.

Women's bodies are led by estrogen as their primary hormone after the onset of puberty. Estrogen is linked to the behaviors of bonding and connection, supporting social skills and observations.

<u>Get Aligned:</u>

Both men and women have benefits from their primary hormones. But we also should be aware of the potential pitfalls that they predispose us to.

Men: Recognize that testosterone leaves you at risk of devaluing connection and cooperation with others.

Women: Recognize a natural tendency to avoid conflict and question your confidence is highly tied to estrogen.

Having awareness of your unique internal programming prepares you for greater success; awareness shines a light on your blind spots as you strive to be a good leader of self.

Week 12, Day 3

<u>Get Inspired:</u>

"The turning points of lives are not the great moments. The real crises are often concealed in occurrences so trivial in appearance that they pass unobserved." — **George Washington**

<u>Get Aligned:</u>

Pay attention to the details, the tiny moments, and everyday engagements. It can be easy to get wrapped up in the big or flashy moments, even if they have little impact on your daily life.

How you engage with your closest tribe day in, and day out <u>matters</u>.

How you live up to your personal moral code when things get tough <u>matters</u>.

How you treat yourself when you are feeling overwhelmed <u>matters</u>.

How you spend and save your money on a daily basis <u>matters</u>.

How you prioritize the tasks and events of your day <u>matters</u>.

What you feed yourself <u>matters</u>.

How and how often you move your body <u>matters</u>.

Each of these "trivial" or tiny choices that we face every day will compound into a picture of who you really are.

Focus on how you chose to show up every single day of your life. Be aware of the choices you are making (or not making) and recognize that they little choices have a big impact on how you will progress along Your Own Journey.

Week 12, Day 4

Get Inspired:

"The culture of any organization is shaped by the worst behavior the leader is willing to tolerate."

-Todd Whitaker

Get Aligned:

YOU are the leader of the 'Organization of You'. You have the final say in what behavior is tolerated or refused. You are setting the tone for how you will run your life. And so it is, therefore, your responsibility to ensure that your worst behaviors are not allowed to fester and diminish the other great parts of you.

Unfortunately, there is incredible pressure in today's society for us to focus on what everyone else thinks and to live by other people's standards. This approach, while it feels popular, will encourage you to exhibit some personal behaviors that are sub-standard for the process of Owning Your Journey.

Act like a CEO. Analyze your behavior from a strategic high level, and work to rectify thoughts, actions, or impulses that will erode the culture of You.

Week 12, Day 5

Get Inspired:

"Telling and finding truth and moving forward cohesively requires a culture of transparency and trust."

-Van Tucker

Get Aligned:

How true these words are for our teams and organizations!

And they are even MORE powerful when applied to our personal functioning.

It is human nature to ignore some of our flaws, to be blind to our challenge areas, and to overcompensate by leaning into our great qualities. If you are to truly be a great leader of self by focusing on Owning Your Journey, then you must identify and reconcile with your truths. You must be brave enough to be fully transparent with yourself and trust in your True North.

Self-awareness is a powerful tool that, when used correctly, leads you to a more fulfilled life. I'm not talking about taking the perfect selfie by perfecting your pose and filter, very much the opposite. I'm talking about truly knowing your triggers and reactions, your biggest dreams and fears, what lights you up and what turns you off, and knowing what type of person you want to be. As you analyze these characteristics you can begin to impact them slowly over time.

None of us will become perfect. That is not the goal.

The goal is to live more aligned with your True North while embracing awareness of your truth so that you can act accordingly.

Week 12, Day 6

Get Inspired:

"I am enough of an artist to draw freely upon my imagination. Imagination is more important than knowledge. Knowledge is limited. Imagination encircles the world."

— Albert Einstein

Get Aligned:

Einstein is largely considered one of the most intelligent men to have lived. And yet, here he is stating that imagination is more important than knowledge. This is because he knew that if we can *imagine* something, we can build it. If we cannot imagine something, how will we ever go about building it?

Let yourself imagine a life that you would love to live. When it is filled with abundance, joy, kindness, positive energy, and aligns with your moral compass you have crafted a good design.

Now your only job is to begin taking tiny steps to build that imaginary world into a reality. That is how you let imagination build your knowledge; you begin to discover what you need to learn, know, or do to bring the imaginative world to life!

But it always begins with a vision …

Week 12, Day 7

Reflect:

What inspired you this week?

What will you carry forward?

Week 13, Day 1

<u>Get Inspired:</u>

Peter Salovey and John Mayer were the first to develop a psychological theory of *Emotional Intelligence* (also referred to as your *Emotional Quotient: EQ*). The pair introduced EQ as a set of skills which they believed helped individuals to accurately "read and express emotions" both in oneself and in others, the ability to "regulate emotions" for self and assisting others, and the ability to "use emotions or feelings" as fuel for planning, motivation, and achievement in your life.

<u>Get Aligned:</u>

Emotional Intelligence is arguably one of the most important skills required to help you find success in your career and in your personal life. As defined above, it has three key features; let's break these down as each component is highly important and equally challenging.

1- **The ability to accurately interpret the emotions of others, and to express yours in a way that others can understand.** This step requires us to put aside our preconceived notions and truly receive the emotional message that others are sharing. It also requires us to acknowledge our emotions, and package them in a way that is legible to others. If we are too aggressive, passive, angry, scattered, or fearful we may not get our message across.

2- **Being able to regulate your emotions (maintain emotional control) and to aid others in their**

emotional control. We all have emotions, but we should not let them get the best of us. We must learn to pause long enough to feel the emotion, and then work through the feelings without letting them control us or send us into rash behavior. Helping others with this step requires modeling the behavior and helping them to understand the process.

3- **Using your feelings / emotions to motivate yourself into action in order to achieve your goals.** This is perhaps the most powerful piece of EQ! When we learn to not only analyze and feel our emotions, but also to use them as motivation, we are able to achieve so much more.

As you work to Own Your Journey, you must reconcile with emotions. We all have them; they come and go throughout each day. When we see them merely as chemical messengers who are trying to get our attention, it becomes easier to analyze them and use them wisely (higher EQ) than to simply react to them without thought (lower EQ). Spend time being aware of your EQ; it will not be time wasted.

Week 13, Day 2

Get Inspired:

"Vulnerability is the birthplace of love, belonging, joy, courage, empathy, and creativity. It is the source of hope, empathy, accountability, and authenticity. If we want greater clarity in our purpose or deeper and more meaningful spiritual lives, vulnerability is the path."

- Brené Brown

Get Aligned:

Vulnerability is possibly one of the most difficult things that we can strive for. We have a deep sense of self-preservation which tells us to "put up a front for protection". However, when we lean into a false façade as a form of avoiding vulnerability, we will continue to be wrapped in armor which prevents us from truly experiencing life in the fullest.

Shedding your armor doesn't make you weak, it makes you brave. It allows you the space to feel life in its fullest capacity. It allows others to know the real you. It makes you authentic, which in turn makes you trustworthy to others.

Bracing or protecting yourself from vulnerable moments becomes a reflex over time; it takes focused effort to change this natural pattern. Be conscious, pay attention, remain self-aware. These are of course the building blocks for all of the steps in Owning Your Journey. Building awareness and comfort in who you are is an essential piece of authentic self-leadership.

Challenge yourself to exhibit small moments of vulnerability by sharing your thoughts, dreams, ideas, and goals. It's ok to start small and build your confidence in this space. Just get started!

Week 13, Day 3

Get Inspired:

Dunbar's Number is a suggested cognitive limit to the number of people with whom one can maintain stable social relationships — relationships in which an individual knows who each person is and how each person relates to every other person. This number was first proposed by British anthropologist Robin Dunbar in his 1993 paper, "Neocortex size as a constraint on group size in primates", as published in the *Journal of Human Evolution*.

Get Aligned:

Dunbar's Number states that 150 people is the maximum size of a group that we can maintain friendships with. It extrapolates to say that five people is the size of your immediately intimate group, and ten people are included in the next level of closeness. The rings grow out from there until it reaches the 150-person limit.

What does this mean for you?

You can't be all things to all people. Some people will forget you in life. Your expansive "network" on social media is not a replacement for real-life connections.

It also means that you should prioritize how you spend your time with your network. Are you neglecting the close five? Are you remembering to interact with the reaches of the 150? Occasionally take stock of how you show up, and ensure you are investing time in the relationships that matter.

Maintaining a level of awareness for how you float through the world and with whom you are connected is a foundational step in Owning Your Journey.

Week 13, Day 4

Get Inspired:

"The essence of leadership is not getting overwhelmed by circumstances."
— Kim Malone Scott

Get Aligned:

To be a good leader of self, we must avoid getting caught up in the minutia of uncomfortable circumstances.

Learn to be a duck, let it roll off your back when things don't go perfectly.

Seek support, find helpers who are better than you at certain tasks, and seek their advice.

Focus on the big picture, there will always be bumps in the road, so learn to keep your eyes on the bigger picture and don't sweat the small stuff.

When we make a show of getting caught up in the little things, we erode the confidence of others in us, we distract them from the big picture, and we fail to support them as a leader.

As a strong leader of self, we stay grounded in our vision for how we want to live our life, and we avoid getting overwhelmed by various circumstances.

Week 13, Day 5

Get Inspired:

"Wherever you go, you can't get rid of yourself."

-Polish Proverb

Get Aligned:

Until you decide to be a person you enjoy being with, you will always feel conflicted.

Be true to yourself. Be honest with yourself. Embrace who you are in your soul.

From this connected space, you will radiate positive energy and will find that you can accomplish so many more of your goals.

~

When you make the effort to connect with yourself, you unknowingly create a positive ripple of energy into the world. When we cease to have that internal battle raging, we free up our energy for more clear communications with others. As your internal connection raises, so does your frequency which allows others to more freely trust in you.

~

Need help getting there?

Check out Equine Facilitated Coaching ... this incredible process uses horses as a mirror to our soul to gently and honestly help us connect with ourselves.

To learn more, check out www.ttwoods.com to discover the power of the Equine Factor.

Week 13, Day 6

Get Inspired:

"Be thankful for what you have; you'll end up having more. If you concentrate on what you don't have, you will never, ever have enough."

– Oprah Winfrey

Get Aligned:

Abundance is an easy concept to grasp, but difficult to hold onto. Believing in abundance means that you are grateful for all that you have, and not fearful that it could disappear. In this state your energy remains open to sharing and to receiving more. You carry a positive cyclical outlook that pays it forward, is grateful for what you currently have, and remains open to receiving in the future.

If you instead are focused on lack, or what you don't have, your energy becomes tight and restrictive. The forward flow stops as it becomes fearful and protective.

If you find yourself focusing on what you DON'T have, be intentional about replacing those thoughts with thoughts of gratitude. That is the key to opening the flow of abundance.

Becoming aware of your energy and leaning into abundance are necessary foundational habits to being a great leader of self.

Week 13, Day 7

Reflect:

What inspired you this week?

What will you carry forward?

Week 14, Day 1

Get Inspired:

Self-determination Theory refers to a person's ability to make choices and manage their own life.

-Edward Deci & Richard Ryan, 1985

Get Aligned:

Let's break this down into easy-to-understand terms...

Self-Determination Theory is a concept stating that our internal motivation is highly associated with creating a purposeful life. And our internal motivation is the key force behind our ability to be good self-leaders. It also states that when we are self-determined we understand that others do not control our life, hence we have the power to shape it.

Therefore, if we listen to our internal motivators, we will be predisposed to creating a purposeful life by being strong self-leaders.

To help drive your ability as a good self-leader, you must know yourself and listen to what motivates you internally. You can then take that drive and harness its power to execute on both enjoyable and required tasks that will create a purposeful life.

Week 14, Day 2

Get Inspired:

"And in the end, it's not the years in your life that count. It's the life in your years."

– Abraham Lincoln

Get Aligned:

If we submit to passing the time each day, to simply going through the motions we are failing ourselves. We are not guaranteed a certain number of years; we must make the most of each day with an energetic mind and open heart.

Good self-leadership is hallmarked by knowing when to push yourself, when to give yourself a break, and when to reignite your inner fire.

~

Be self-aware by doing a daily personal check-in:

Am I of positive mind?

Am I exuding energy?

Am I putting positive vibes into the world?

Do I need to refuel myself?

~

Awareness is the first step on the journey of self-leadership. It cannot be skipped.

Week 14, Day 3

Get Inspired:

Maslow's Hierarchy of Needs is an idea in psychology proposed by American psychologist Abraham Maslow in his 1943 paper "A Theory of Human Motivation". The theory is a classification system designed to outline the general needs of society with the base representing the most elementary of needs that we all have, then proceeding to more acquired emotions at the top of the pyramid.

Get Aligned:

The pyramid starts at the base as most urgent and rises to the top. A more modern and simpler version of the pyramid includes:

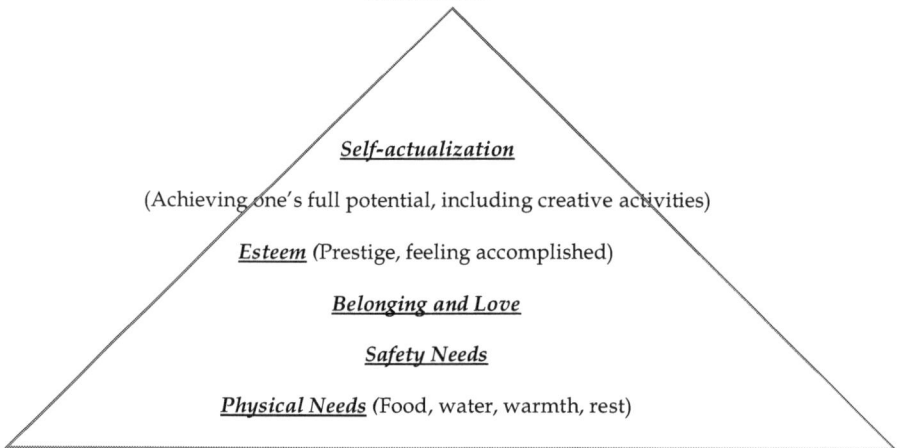

Self-actualization

(Achieving one's full potential, including creative activities)

Esteem (Prestige, feeling accomplished)

Belonging and Love

Safety Needs

Physical Needs (Food, water, warmth, rest)

According to this pyramid, we must fulfill our basic physical needs and safety needs before we can expend any energy on belonging and love. As you flow up the pyramid, we find that achieving your full potential lives at the top of the pyramid. If we look at this through a lens of self-leadership, we will need to work our way up to self-actualization. We must "take care of our house" before we can begin to seek the finishing details.

If you are lacking in any of the first three categories, you will likely find it difficult to find peace with esteem or self-actualization.

Week 14, Day 4

Get Inspired:

"Listen to the whispers and you won't have to hear the screams."

-Cherokee saying

Get Aligned:

When we ignore the tiny sounds around us that something isn't working, these signs will generally escalate until we can no longer avoid the issue.

Have you ever been in a relationship that had tiny problems which you kept ignoring, until the entire relationship blew up?

Have you ever heard the rumors at work, and eventually they turned into a full-blown scandal?

Have you ever had that toddler who is tired/cranky/hungry as you determinedly motored through the grocery store, only to be faced with a hurricane level tantrum in the middle of isle 22?

The universe has a way of getting our attention if we fail to listen when it whispers to us. Without fail. Every Single Time.

When I was working my full-time corporate job and simultaneously raising two tiny humans, I was crushing it at night preparing to get my consulting business off the ground. But in reality, I was slowly breaking. I was exhausted, overworked, overstressed, and overwhelmed. I knew I needed a break, but instead kept driving forward to an arbitrary deadline I had set for myself.

When I wouldn't listen to the whispers of my body telling me to rest, it started screaming at me. I started having "mysterious" symptoms which included my body literally forcing me to shut down; I couldn't stand up, lift my head, or move without becoming violently ill or passing out. My heart rate and blood pressure would get cemented at basement levels, for days.

Doctors put me through batteries of tests; once we determined that I was "normal" I felt like a fraud, because in my core, I knew the problem was me.

I have since slowly learned to listen better to my body. Truthfully, I still have them a few times per year. But now I do a better job to heed the warning signs that show up as whispers when I get dangerously close to my next breakdown; and sometimes I am diligent enough to rest and avoid the calamity.

What whispers are you ignoring in your life? They will eventually show up as screams if you don't stop and listen.

Awareness of self is the bedrock to Owning Your Journey.

Week 14, Day 5

Get Inspired:

"The measure of success is not whether you have a tough problem to deal with, but whether it is the same problem you had last year."

-John Foster Dulles

Get Aligned:

Are you on the hamster wheel? Meaning, do you continue to SAY that you are addressing the same problem or challenge repeatedly, only to make no progress?

Take a time out.

Evaluate what you have been doing, and what is NOT working. Consider what you could do differently. Honestly acknowledge if you are doing to the work, investing in the micro habits, and staying committed to the process … or if you are all lip service.

If you are stuck on solving a problem, go back to the model of self-leadership to determine where your gap is:

1- Do you have the vision to see what exactly you are trying to solve for?
2- Do you have the mindset to positively pursue the goal?
3- Do you have the right tools to show up productively? The right support, the right plan, and the right process?
4- Are you executing consistently? Or are you lagging behind?

Sometimes, the greatest gift we can give ourselves on the path to improvement is to invest in a Coach to help us see our blind spots and to hold us accountable. Maybe you have a partner or friend who can do this for you (although, this can be challenging due to the nature of personal relationships). Maybe you have a mentor who can assist you. Or maybe it's time to work with a Coach.

Pinpoint the breakdown in the process and give yourself the support mechanism needed to solve the problem ... or agree to let it go.

Start with awareness.

Week 14, Day 6

Get Inspired:

"The longest journey is the journey inward."

– Dag Hannarskjold

Get Aligned:

It is fun cruising through life during the good times; yet those seasons rarely teach us about ourselves and our strengths. But when we experience a challenge, we come face to face with who we are under pressure.

Do you like what you see? Or do you want to make changes?

Do you rise to the occasion, or do you shrink back, lash out, run away, or act recklessly?

Getting real about how you react, and how you WANT to react is the first step to change. Keep a log of your challenges and focus on your reactions. Vow to adjust your mindset, and then your actions will follow.

In short, know yourself.

Week 14, Day 7

Reflect:

What inspired you this week?

What will you carry forward?

Week 15, Day 1

Get Inspired:

"Ritual is important to us as human beings. It ties us to our traditions and out histories."

-Miller Williams

Get Aligned:

The human ability to be creative, to adapt, and to pivot is powerful and unique. We must not stifle these feelings and ideas when they come to us; sometimes they will impact our ability to not just survive but also to thrive.

If you are feeling stuck as you navigate your Own Journey, maybe it is time to adjust or reconsider your rituals. Are you overly focused on work or study, without time to be creative, engage with others, or simply rest? Rituals can be incredibly helpful to us, but if we don't occasionally examine them, we risk continuing with behaviors or time commitments that no longer serve us in the current season of life.

It is OK to admit that what served you five years ago no longer serves you today. Observe, adjust, and move forward.

Begin by being aware.

Week 15, Day 2

<u>Get Inspired:</u>

There are four key communication styles or preferences, as outlined through the **Everything DiSC®** programs by John Wiley & Sons, Inc.

These communication preferences give us insights into how we connect with others, where we can have communication breakdowns, and how to find deeper connections to those around us. The four key styles include:

D-Dominant

i-Influence

S-Steadiness

C-Conscientious

<u>Get Aligned:</u>

Knowing your communication preferences will help you to connect on a deeper level with others, and to reduce the number of frustrations that stem from miscommunications. If you stop to consider the challenges and disruptions to your day (both personally and professionally), most conflicts or problems arise from some form of miscommunication … people not hearing each other or not understanding each other clearly.

The 4 DiSC® styles each have distinct comfort zones relating to how outgoing or reserved they are, and to how task verses people oriented they are.

Being flexible in how you communicate is a superpower! You can get other people's attention by simply approaching any conversation (written, oral or otherwise) in a manner that makes the message clear and comfortable for the intended audience. Knowing how we appear to others when we communicate and combining that with knowing how others naturally *prefer* to be communicated with will unlock next-level connection.

I share the concept with my clients in this manner: Communicating with someone else in a flexible manner is like dressing appropriately for a party. If it is a black-tie event, you don't have to show up in an enormous Barbie-Ballgown, but you *should* be dressier than yoga pants and flip flops! Remain true to your personal style, but in a way which reflects that you read the party invitation and respect the guidelines of the hosts!

Having awareness of how you show up is a sign that you are focused on Owning Your Journey.

~

To learn more about DiSC® styles or to get a personal assessment set up for you or your team, reach out to Stacy at www.ttwoods.com.

Week 15, Day 3

<u>Get Inspired:</u>

"We're all water from different rivers, that's why it's so easy to meet; we're all water in this vast, vast ocean, someday we'll evaporate together."

– Yoko Ono

<u>Get Aligned:</u>

What an incredible image to visualize, us as water and us all eventually evaporating together! It is a reminder that we are all built of the same building blocks, and that during our time on earth we are privileged to exercise our individual tendencies, preferences, and creativity.

With this visual, two key questions come to mind:

1. What are you doing with that ability to choose or express your preferences?
2. Are you maximizing your connection to others?

For the first, part of what makes us human is our independent thinking ability. Self-leadership demands that we build this skill as we consider how we want to live and where we want to focus our time. Do you want to climb the traditional ladder at work; do you want to stay in your current role, becoming a master at your responsibilities; or do you want to explore as many departments/industries/companies as possible while you learn to become a business chameleon? There is no correct answer. As we pursue an authentic journey for ourselves, we should be asking and answering those questions on a regular basis. And we should be sharing our goals with our supervisors to engage their support in developing a productive plan to get there. Don't have a supervisor who will support you? No problem, seek a supportive mentor or coach, or seek a role within a new company that is a better fit for you.

For the second question, how connected are you to those around you? While we are all different and unique, as Yoko reminds us, we are also all connected at the most basic level. When we look past surface differences to see the common ground among us, we learn new skills and benefit from the broad variety of viewpoints. At work, encourage the "quiet person" to share their thoughts, invite an intern to lunch, or connect with a colleague across the country/globe over virtual coffee.

Do not only surround yourself with replicas of yourself; challenge yourself to seek out and know people with different backgrounds, appearances, experiences, and beliefs. They do not need to be your inner circle, but they will keep you open to growth as you pursue your Own Journey.

Week 15, Day 4

<u>Get Inspired:</u>

"The cure for boredom is curiosity. There is no cure for curiosity."

-Dorothy Parker

<u>Get Aligned:</u>

Curiosity may have killed the cat, but it gave him an interesting life!

Humans are designed as puzzle solvers, it's literally in our DNA, strongly imprinted from paleolithic times and earlier.

Tap into your natural curiosity by trying something new or reading a non-fiction book. If you fail to feed this side of your brain, you risk it becoming weak.

Besides, life is more fun when you approach it with curiosity as opposed to ignorance or irritation.

~

Build a tribe of curious friends.

Suggest a game / trivia night to get the juices flowing. Set up regular brainstorming sessions at work so that everyone is encouraged to view challenges from a new perspective.

Curiosity is a state of being that anyone can choose to adopt.

Week 15, Day 5

Get Inspired:

I will love the light for it shows me the way, yet I will endure the darkness because it shows me the stars."

– Og Mandino

Get Aligned:

A vision or dream for our future is a gift to behold. What do we do, then, if we are in a time of darkness and no vision is coming to us?

Do not panic. You are normal! Like all things in life, visions and dreams come in spurts and seasons. There will be times when you are so filled with purpose, focus, sadness, or illness that visions are not coming to you. During these times, do not fret. The darkness is a valid season and often leads to new visions beyond your wildest imagination!

Week 15, Day 6

Get Inspired:

"If you can dream it, you can do it."

-Walt Disney

Get Aligned:

Walt Disney had an incredible dream. One where he would create a theme park beyond the current experience of Disneyland; it would be bigger, better, and more futuristic. And so, he set on a quest to build Disney World.

To protect his dream, he began buying plats of land under various business names. He worked with his brother to visualize the project, which included EPCOT (the Experimental Prototype Community of Tomorrow).

Sadly, Walt died before the project was finished. However, to protect and support Walt's vision, his brother Roy insisted that the project be finished, and that the name officially included Walt's name in it as a memorial to his brother's plans.

Walt's vision to create something mesmerizing was indeed realized; In 2018, Walt Disney World was the most visited vacation resort in the world.

If you have that burning fire of a dream, find your trusted tribe and gather their support for your efforts in making it a reality. There is no stopping you if you refuse to give up!

Week 15, Day 7

Reflect:

What inspired you this week?

What will you carry forward?

PART 2:

Align Your Mindset

"You must learn a new way to think before you can master a new way to be."

-*Marianne Williamson*

Week 16, Day 1

Get Inspired:

Mindset is defined by *Oxford Languages* as:

"The established set of attitudes held by someone."

Get Aligned:

Mindset is crucial to our success as we work towards Owning Our Journey. Mindset is the ability to choose our set of attitudes, and this means that we can and should choose a mindset that supports the belief in our visions. If we don't like the path we have been on, if we find that we are too trenched in the negative/ not enough/ lack mindset ... we can adjust our mindset by changing our attitudes.

Sounds hard, right?!

Well, to be honest, it is. But why would we let others impact our mindset when we have the power to drive the direction of this bus?

To begin, take time to be aware of your mindset; are you a 'glass-half-full' kind of person, or a 'glass-half-empty' kind of person? Do you default to excuses or blaming others, or do you step up and take ownership (maybe too often)? Do you believe that your win is not someone else's loss, or does their success reduce your opportunity in life? Take your own temperature to see what attitudes you carry in your mind. A negative mindset will always block your progress towards your vision/goals.

From there, decide what (if anything) you would like to change about your mindset. The most basic - and powerful - place to being is the process of moving from a *Lack Mindset* to an *Abundant Mindset*. We slowly train our brains to look for the good, the opportunity, and the abundance in every situation. In a sense, we are reprogramming our mainframe computer away from the negative and scarce thoughts, and towards the land of opportunity.

This process takes time, and intentional practice. But it is available to anyone who wishes to grow in their ability to lead themselves.

A few tips to help you maximize this transformation:

1- **Create a visual**. Select a word, a phrase, or an image that evokes abundance for you. Place it on a sticky-note at your laptop. Paint it on your bathroom mirror in washable paint. Tape it to your car dashboard. Just put it in a place that you will SEE and READ every day.

2- **Read a mantra**. Develop a sentence (or two) that describes the positive and grateful mindset that you want to embody and/or the goals from your vision that you are working towards. Print it up and position this in a place where you can read it every single day.

3- **Write your thoughts**. Keep a journal with your thoughts as you grow into this positive mindset. Keep a log of your activity or progress in your planner, tracking your commitment to an abundant mindset.

Week 16, Day 2

Get Inspired:

"Life is like riding a bicycle. To keep your balance, you must keep moving."
— Albert Einstein

Get Aligned:

Do you remember learning to ride a bike? First came the training wheels, the safety precaution that kept us from falling. And then the big day arrived when we removed the training wheels. It felt like learning to ride all over again! We had become reliant on those tiny support wheels and could stop whenever we were nervous. Suddenly, we had to keep pedaling to stay upright.

Our first child learned to ride a bike this way. I can clearly recall the day that the training wheels came off. She was almost 5 years old, and she had to trust her power to stay afloat. This child has always been a determined daredevil, so it was no surprise that she embraced it quickly after a few moments of hesitation and encouragement to keep pedaling.

Can kids learn to ride a bike without the support of an adult? Of course, but it is much harder.

Who is the one to encourage you to keep pedaling as an adult?

Sometimes we panic when it gets hard and look down at the ground … only to quickly fall there.

What if you had someone to remind you to:

-Keep your eyes up

-Keep pedaling

-Look where you want to go

-Breathe

-And have fun!

You can be that person for yourself, but if you are really good at self-leadership, you will also find that cheerleader and coach to support you on your journey!

Week 16, Day 3

<u>Get Inspired:</u>

"The book you don't read won't help."

-Jim Rohn

<u>Get Aligned:</u>

There are a variety of options to gain new knowledge. Traditional books, e-readers, audible books, podcasts, videos, blogs, and more. If you are not taking in knowledge by actively seeking one of these avenues, then you are falling behind. Failing to continue learning in life is a clear choice to wither on the vine.

You may not always pick up your favorite book, but you will always learn something!

Make ingesting content part of your daily routine. Try listening while walking or driving, try reading or watching videos before bed, consider a quick blog over lunch.

For a list of my favorite books, follow me on LinkedIn (*@Stacy-Best-Wood*), or visit my website for more information (www.ttwoods.com).

Week 16, Day 4

Get Inspired:

"A man is but a product of his thoughts. What he thinks he becomes."

-Gandhi

Get Aligned:

The Law of Attraction resurfaces here. Many great leaders in life have recognized its importance and shared the concept with in their own voice and style.

Gandhi reminds us that our thoughts are powerful. They influence our actions and our belief systems. They are the subtle seeds that we sow to become the crops that we harvest.

Be clear and honest in your thoughts. If they are negative, doubtful, steeped in lack, or in anger please pause to reflect. How can you make a shift and align your thoughts with the person and life you want to live?

~

If you are keeping bad company, it's time for a change.

Be that change by distancing yourself from the toxic or negative people in your life. You don't owe them an explanation, but you are welcome to provide insight into your desire to lean into a more positive space.

We are highly influenced by those around us, their words can easily become our thoughts ... which in turn becomes who we are. Choose wisely.

Week 16, Day 5

Get Inspired:

"If you only read the books that everyone else is reading, you can only think what everyone else is thinking."
— Haruki Murakami

Get Aligned:

Becoming an independent thinker is not accidental. We work at this effort by taking in a variety of information; opinions that we both agree and disagree with. We read, listen, write, explore, and draw to pull in inspiration. We challenge our own points of view, and we defend our points of view.

Being an independent thinker means that you will develop the skills to work through any tough decision in life. You will learn to analyze the data, ask for more information, and to listen to your gut instinct. Once you can combine these habits you will have an easier time Owning Your Journey because you are able to clearly see how a choice aligns with or conflicts with your purpose and goals.

In a world where the popular or careful opinion prevails, don't be afraid to think for yourself.

Week 16, Day 6

<u>Get Inspired:</u>

"To increase your passion, do the following: Take your temperature. How passionate are you about your life and work? … Return to your first love. Evaluate your life and career in light of those old loves. … Associate with people of passion. … Passion is contagious."

-**John C. Maxwell**, *The 21 Indispensable Qualities of a Leader*, Thomas Nelsen Publishers, 1999, pg. 86-87.

<u>Get Aligned:</u>

Letting passion die in our lives is like watching fruit shrivel on the vine, it's a waste. If you are feeling less than passionate, follow Maxwell's advice above to reignite the spark.

In this moment, list a few things that you are (or used to be) truly passionate about. Now outline how you can or do incorporate them into your life on a daily basis.

Per Maxwell, passion is contagious. Share your passion with your tribe and seek out passionate people to engage with.

Week 16, Day 7

<u>Reflect:</u>

What inspired you this week?

What will you carry forward?

Week 17, Day 1

Get Inspired:

"Let us use this gift of Nature and count it among the greatest things."

-**Seneca**, *Moral Letters* 119.15b

Get Aligned:

If you are missing out on the abundance of Nature, you are turning a blind eye to an incredible teacher. In Nature, we are motivated by learning key lessons of leadership, we are inspired by sights that we cannot replicate as humans, we are encouraged by beautiful sounds, we are delighted by complex puzzles to solve, we are grounded in the very earth that we came from, and we are encouraged by the possibility of tomorrow.

As you find your comfort level with Nature, you will tap into a deeper vessel of learning than you thought possible. Nature will help to shape your mindset; you will be encouraged to remain curious, awe filled, energized, and committed to your vision.

Come in touch with Nature at least once each day and consider sharing the inspiration you gained with someone in your life.

Week 17, Day 2

Get Inspired:

"I don't think of all the misery, but of the beauty that still remains."

-Anne Frank

Get Aligned:

If Anne Frank could see beauty and opportunities through her traumas, then we all can. Where we set our mind is our reality.

Focus your energy not on the negative, but on the beauty of what is yet to come. Train your brain to be a positive thinker by redirecting your negative thoughts as you catch them.

Put good into this world through your thoughts and your words.

Week 17, Day 3

<u>Get Inspired:</u>

"The alternative to growing old is not good."

-Elmer Albert Allen, *my grandfather*

<u>Get Aligned:</u>

My grandfather had an incredibly difficult childhood which included being turned over to an orphanage by his own father because his stepmother did not want him, from which he eventually ran away at the age of 13 … living on his own in the streets.

Given these circumstances, he was not a formally educated man with a higher education but was one of the most insightful men I knew. This is one of his many sayings (which admittedly I may have slightly skewed his words, but they remain in spirit). He was essentially telling us that if we avoid growing old, the only alternative is to die young.

As a society, we have a collective fear of aging. We spend countless dollars trying to avoid 'looking old'. We shun the thought of becoming "a senior citizen". I, too, battle with the pressures of looking young as I age. I try to remind myself of the amazing things that this body has experienced and done for me. However, I know that in today's world, this is a constant battle and a discussion we must repeat in our minds often.

We sometimes forget that with age comes wisdom and a vast landscape of adventures realized. If we can adjust our mindset to embrace the knowledge that comes with age, maybe we won't fear it as much. Maybe we will instead respect it and embrace wherever we are on the path.

Find a "senior citizen" in your life and listen to their stories. The wisdom and perspectives they have gained may surprise you!

Week 17, Day 4

Get Inspired:

"Sometimes your joy is the source of your smile, but sometimes your smile can be the source of your joy."
— Thich Nhat Hanh

Get Aligned:

Sometimes joy is presented to us. And sometimes we must create our own joy.

You have the power to both embrace and to create a joyous mindset.

Know what lights up your soul and do something each day to ignite that spark so that it may never go dark.

Share your light. Be the source of a smile on someone's lips or a song in their heart.

Week 17, Day 5

Get Inspired:

"Humans have brains that are sensitive to social and emotional stress, and we always have. Perhaps what matters is not the source of the stress but the ability to recover from it. This is a key point, because it's perhaps what we've lost by giving up our connections to [Nature]. It's hard not to feel the pull of a grounded reality when you're dipping into a muddy trail or a flowing river."

-Florence Williams, *The Nature Fix*, W.W. Norton & Company, 2017, pg.45

Get Aligned:

Stress is not a new phenomenon; but as a species we are struggling to survive the stress in our lives. As a society, we are experiencing high rates of stress-induced health disorders and complications.

However, when we make space to connect with the earth and Nature around us, we improve our ability to recover from stress. Our most natural and abundant resource of stress-relief is free, and all around us; it is found by simply creating space to connect back with the most basic elements of Nature. This is how our ancestors mentally survived incredibly stressful lives as hunter and gatherers, where the death rate was high, and safety was scare.

Reducing our stress to a manageable level is in alignment with your quest for self-leadership. It is not anyone else's responsibility to manage our stress … it is ours alone. This is directly tied to our mindset. A healthy and productive mindset will be eroded by untamed stress.

Choose to improve your stress-recovery-ratio. Make dedicated time on your calendar to experience Nature in a quiet and absorbable manner. Watch a sunrise/sunset, walk barefoot in the park, splash in the ocean or in a creek, go for a hike, or lay on a blanket and watch the stars.

Week 17, Day 6

Get Inspired:

"We all step in shit from time to time. We hit roadblocks, we
fuck up, we get fucked, we get sick, we don't get what we
want, we cross thousands of "could have done betters" and
"wish that wouldn't have happeneds" in life. Stepping in shit
is inevitable, so let's either see it as good luck, or figure out
how to do it less often."
— **Matthew McConaughey**, *Greenlights*

Get Aligned:

If we aren't learning from our mistakes we are merely fools.

None of us would have learned to walk without falling a
million times and getting up to try again.

Analyze your mistakes, figure out what went wrong and what
you could do better next time (not what others did wrong).
Hold onto that thought and apply it in the future when you
get stuck.

Take ownership of your mistakes and release blame from
others. You will sleep better at night, and they will likely
ruminate on it longer.

Week 17, Day 7

<u>Reflect:</u>

What inspired you this week?

What will you carry forward?

Week 18, Day 1

Get Inspired:

"Everyone knows what attention is. It is the taking possession by the mind…"

"Without selective interest, experience is an utter chaos."

-**James, Henry**. (1890). *The principles of psychology, Vol. 1.* Henry Holt and Co.

James went on to divide attention into two categories:

Voluntary or active attention (when we are attending to tasks) and

Involuntary or reflex attention (a demand on our focus such as a loud noise, a text alert, or a flash of lights).

Get Aligned:

The lessons from James allow us to realize that we are being pulled between both Voluntary and Involuntary attention each day. Staying on task is hard work because the Involuntary is constantly striving to interrupt the Voluntary. Add into this formula the high frequency of modern Involuntary alerts each day (text messages, emails, social media alerts, etc.) and you can easily see why it is difficult to stay grounded in the Voluntary attention space.

To improve our ability to stay focused, we must dilute the noise and distractions around us. We must be crystal clear about what we are focusing on. And we must protect this space by creating a functional environment in which to purse this quest of Voluntary attention.

~

Carve out time on your calendar for some focused work. Create quiet by turning off all notifications from each of your devices and setting a timer for the length of focus you are pursuing.

Create Voluntary time to focus on your family each evening by automatically turning your phone to "do not disturb" for an hour or two. Making your family/friends a priority is never wasted time.

Week 18, Day 2

<u>Get Inspired:</u>

"Attention is everything; Without it, we don't see, hear, taste. Your brain keeps track of about four things at once. How do you prioritize what's important and what's not? Through inhibition. …We have far more information than the brain can deal with. Most of what the brain is doing is filtering, tuning stuff out so we can focus in on things that are relevant."

-Paul Atchley

As quoted within The Nature Fix, Florence Williams, pg. 43.

<u>Get Aligned:</u>

Our brains are on a constant system overload. These advanced computers of ours are working overtime to filter out what they think is less important.

The ability to change our programming lies within each of us! We can determine what information makes it through to our conscious mind, and what is let go. To do so, we simply need to focus on that which matters.

Give our attention to the things that are important. This selective process will improve our processing systems so that when we invest more attention in a high priority topic, we will begin to naturally notice these things more frequently in the future.

What matters to you?

Stop filling your brain with noise and start focusing on the important stuff!

Be clear on what is important so that you can consciously direct your brain power to those topics.

Week 18, Day 3

Get Inspired:

"Give thanks for unknown blessings already on their way."

-Native American saying

Get Aligned:

Gratitude is the source of all that is good. When we lean into gratitude it is impossible to simultaneously be angry, scared, selfish, bitter, jealous, nervous, or depressed. In that moment of gratitude, we are in a state of peace which is induced by acknowledging all that is good in our lives.

Some people pray, some mediate on their blessings, and some simply thank the Universe for the good. There is not a right or wrong way to do it, as long as you do it regularly.

To get started, I recommend you pick a specific time of day that works for you. Some popular choices include: as soon as you wake up in the morning, while brushing teeth, before a meal, before bed, or as you are falling asleep (my personal favorite). Spontaneous moments of gratitude are also encouraged, but if this is new for you its best to plan a time so that you don't forget.

From there, simply state: "I am grateful for ...", and list as many or as few things that you are truly grateful for. I begin with the same core list each day, and then add on other thoughts as they come to me.

The more you practice, the more you will crave this exercise because of the joy and peace that it brings to you, even amid chaos. When we learn to cultivate a grateful and relaxed mindset, it opens us up to see opportunities that we may have otherwise been blind to. Gratitude is the process of fertilizing the "fields" in our brain so that we can grow a healthy mindset.

~

Teach your children to be grateful, incorporate this practice into family time. Start simply by asking your family to share 1-3 things they are thankful for each day.

In the office, consider an anonymous gratitude jar where employees are encouraged to contribute throughout the year or quarter. Take time to publicly read the contributions at the end of a given period.

Week 18, Day 4

Get Inspired:

"In your actions, don't procrastinate. In your conversations, don't confuse. In your thoughts, don't wander. In your soul, don't be passive or aggressive. In your life, don't be all about business."

-Marcus Aurelius, *Meditations* 8.51

Get Aligned:

I believe what Marcus is trying to share with us is the simple act of being present.

Being PRESENT is simple in concept, but often so hard in application.

We cannot change what has already happened, we waste energy stressing over what may happen in the future. When we do these things, we are frivolously wasting energy and detracting from the most important moment in our lives: the present.

Work to catch yourself as you stray from center. Make it a habit to come back to the present as often as you stray in your mind. This muscle takes time to build, but you can improve your abilities, and therefore your self-leadership ability.

Week 18, Day 5

Get Inspired:

"Fairly simple brain training ... or methods of thinking, can carve new pathways in our adult brains, pathways that encourage resilience, or confident thinking, and that then become part of our hard-wiring. ... [however], The most dramatic examples of a change in the brain's function and structure have involved basic meditation."

-Katty Kay and Claire Shipman, *The Confidence Code*, Harper Collins Publishers, 2014, pg. 78-79

Get Aligned:

Unless you have been living under a rock for the past decade, you have surely heard that meditation is great for you on many levels.

Our ability to positively impact how we think is profound in our ability to thrive. Gone are the days of being a prisoner to your thoughts; take control and begin to shape how you process information, how you show up, and how you want to reflect on this world.

If you are struggling to get started, download one of many apps that can guide you, listen to a meditation podcast or YouTube video, or find a friend who can help you. Take control of your mindset through the practice of meditation.

Week 18, Day 6

Get Inspired:

"So, when a person loses their composure it isn't their skills and virtues that are troubled, but the spirit in which they exist, and when that spirit calms down so do those things."

-**Epictetus**, *Discourses*, 3.3.21-22

Get Aligned:

You will get flustered, and you will make mistakes in life. Take heart in knowing that these moments are fleeting, and they do not define you.

Instead, remind yourself that this is but a moment in time, and your spirit is excited out of frustration.

Take 10 deep breaths or go for a short walk, and then you will begin to see the way forward. If you feel the rise of emotion and lean into it, there is nothing but more trouble on the other side.

Bringing your mindset back to a logic centered space is an essential skill of good self-leadership. Don't become a slave to your emotions.

Week 18, Day 7

Reflect:

What inspired you this week?

What will you carry forward?

Week 19, Day 1

<u>Get Inspired:</u>

"You're only a victim to the degree of what your perception allows."

- Shannon L. Alder

<u>Get Aligned:</u>

Victimhood is a mindset.

It's time to drop the victim mentality. It is a dangerous and dead-end road. If you struggle to let this go, please get professional therapy to help you shed the burden.

Don't be so egotistical to assume that everything is directed at you; that is an immature and selfish way to live.

Once you let go of playing the victim, you will see endless opportunities for learning or growth that come from the tough or negative situations. You cannot afford to fall down the well of self-pity on your road to Owning Your Journey.

Week 19, Day 2

Get Inspired:

"Wholehearted living is ... going to bed at night thinking, 'Yes, I am imperfect and vulnerable and sometimes afraid, but that doesn't change the truth that I am also brave and worth of love and belonging.'."

- Brené Brown, *Daring Greatly*, Gotham Books, 2012, pg. 10.

Get Aligned:

We must love ourselves, trust ourselves, and show up as our whole selves to live wholeheartedly. Adapting a wholehearted mindset is the basic entry fee for planning to Own Your Journey.

If you are ready to do this work, read or listen to some of Brené Brown's research in this area.

~

Practical ways to practice Wholehearted Living:

As a parent: Don't try to be good or bad, but instead try to be engaged and pay close attention to what the children are doing and seeing.

As a leader at work: Create space for failure so that risks can be taken, and lessons can be learned.

Week 19, Day 3

Get Inspired:

"Education is not the learning of facts, but the training of the mind to think!"

– Albert Einstein

Get Aligned:

How true this is! As a parent with young children, I have learned this lesson a million times! School is not about memorizing items for a test; it is about learning to process the information and make sense of it.

When we shift from the burden of memorizing facts and into the space of understanding the story, we will find delight in the process of education. And education does not end with school. We should be constantly learning and growing as adults.

If you are not currently learning daily, you are at risk of letting your brain get bored and stale. Listen to podcasts, read/listen to books, play games, work puzzles; each of these activities will give your brain new information that it must assimilate into a story that it can recall. Continually challenging our brains is key to remaining sharp both in our career growth and in our overall youthfulness as we age.

Adopting a growth mindset will support your efforts as you seek to Own Your Journey.

Week 19, Day 4

Get Inspired:

"Success is the ability to go from one failure to another with no loss of enthusiasm."

– Winston Churchill

Get Aligned:

Success is often talked about as the pinnacle for which we all strive. But what is it really? I believe that tangible success is different for each of us, and we won't know when we've reached it unless we are clear about what we want to achieve/experience in this lifetime.

However, Churchill's definition of success is more about a state of mind than a tangible space. The concept that we can maintain a successful state of mind by simply not getting bogged down by the challenges of life is empowering. That means that each of us can find success every single day of our lives if we choose to do so. Success is the ability to keep a positive and enthusiastic outlook. If we can do that, we will surely live in contentment and fulfillment as we explore our Own Journey through life.

Week 19, Day 5

Get Inspired:

"What I most want you to understand is that your body is continuously and convincingly sending messages to your brain, and you get to control the content of those messages."

-Amy Cuddy

Get Aligned:

Most of us are stuck on autopilot, allowing negative or fearful thoughts to take over without putting up a fight. These thoughts are the ones that drive us to feel a nagging lack of confidence; the ones that take up residence in your head with no effort or backbone; the ones that are heavy like a wet blanket.

What would happen if we purposefully directed our thoughts to a more productive space? What if we told ourselves we ARE capable, strong, smart, ready, fearless? Would we then be willing to step up, take a risk, share our voice, be a leader, wear the bikini, sport the dread locks, run for office, finish our degree, start a blog, or try something new?

If we have the choice as to what messages we send to our brains, WHY don't we put effort into sending *positive* messages?

We have become so habituated to the space of "lack", that we often don't see how easy it is to embrace abundantly positive thoughts.

Let's begin today. Purposefully tell yourself something inspiring, motivating, or affirmational about yourself or your abilities. Repeat it often and with intention until you believe it! Let this place of an abundant and positive mindset become your new normal.

Week 19, Day 6

Get Inspired:

"Life isn't about waiting for the storm to pass…It's about learning to dance in the rain."

– Vivian Greene

Get Aligned:

Storms will come and go throughout our lives. There is no avoiding it. It is nature's way of cleansing, creating a fresh start, and of unleashing her powers.

So it is also with our lives; the storms we face may be physical, emotional, or mental. Each of them challenges us in a new way and pushes us to a humble awareness, to new beginnings, and to personal growth.

Rain can be a delightful playground. Do you remember as a child stomping in puddles or standing face in the rain in order to feel it pelting down on your face? Let's not lose that innocence.

Don't be afraid of getting wet; jump right into the messy puddle and look the rainclouds in the face. Often that simple change of perspective takes a situation from being a miserable experience to a fun or fresh experience. Our perspective is our reality. If you merely change your perspective by approaching a challenge from a different angle, you might be surprised by what you discover!

The next time you face a mishap, let's say the new carton of milk goes flying and splatters every corner of your kitchen …

pause to decide if it's a real storm, or merely a chance to laugh and dance in the mud puddle.

Week 19, Day 7

Reflect:

What inspired you this week?

What will you carry forward?

Week 20, Day 1

Get Inspired:

"This life is what you make it. No matter what, you're going to mess up sometimes, it's a universal truth. But the good part is you get to decide how you're going to mess it up."

-Marilyn Monroe

Get Aligned:

If we were to stop taking ourselves so seriously and stop being afraid of messing up, we would find the freedom to accomplish so much more in life.

When we embrace the concept that we ARE going to make mistakes, it becomes much easier to flow into a space of failing forward: the process of trying, failing, learning from your mistakes, and trying again with a new approach.

Week 20, Day 2

Get Inspired:

"I like nonsense, it wakes up the brain cells. Fantasy is a necessary ingredient in living."

— Dr. Seuss

Get Aligned:

Don't color in the lines. Don't limit yourself to what you already know. Don't hold back your silly side.

There is a time and a place for strait laced thinking and behavior, but if you find yourself in a rut it is time to call upon your nonsense brain to get you out of a jam.

A very simple place to start and find inspiration is by reading one of the great Dr. Suess books! Honestly.

The shear nonsensical prose will twist your brain into a space of "what-if" and help you to claim back some creativity. This creativity will serve as the source for an openminded approach to Your Journey and Your Life.

Week 20, Day 3

Get Inspired:

"Live as if you were to die tomorrow. Learn as if you were to live forever."

— Mahatma Gandhi

Get Aligned:

Curiosity is your greatest friend on the path to Owning Your Journey.

Curiosity drives you to ask *why*, to seek answers, to consider different viewpoints or different approaches to solve a problem. It allows you to be humble, to try again, and to improve.

We were all born with a need to be curious and learn. That internal drive gets dampened in many adults as they move into the monotonous routine of working. The good news is that you can resurrect that innate drive to learn! Commit to learning something new each day. Like all habits, start small so that you will stay committed to the process, and you can add on as you grow in curiosity.

~

Ideas to get you started:

- Commit to logging five minutes on a foreign language app each day.
- Listen to a podcast or audible book as you commute to work or workout.

- Take up a new hobby such as gardening/painting/yoga.
- Explore new recipes to cook for dinner each night.

Let curiosity become the new status quo for your mindset, and it will take you to places that you never expected you might reach!

Week 20, Day 4

Get Inspired:

"In three words I can sum up everything I've learned about life: it goes on."

— Robert Frost

Get Aligned:

It can be easy to get caught up in the drama of ourselves. When things aren't going right or are difficult, we tend to feel as though the world is crashing down around us. In reality, the world rarely cares or notices for more than a moment … and life keeps marching forward.

Personally, I tend to get stuck on a repeat cycle of worry in my mind after I feel as though I have let someone down or when someone is upset with me. Those are the two toughest spots that I struggle to dig out of. I have found that to move forward, I need to follow this formula when I get stuck on the wheel of worry:

1- Reminding myself of the facts in the situation.
2- Delivering a proper apology (when appropriate).
3- Do a quick refresh of "why I'm not a horrible person" in my own brain, as often as needed.

When I do these three things, I eventually can move on with less worry.

Only *you* can ensure that you don't get hung up on a past relationship, a slight that you may have encountered, a failed attempt at a goal, a public embarrassment, being passed for a promotion, or some other version of NO that has impacted your life. Of course, we may all need some time to lick our wounds, but at some point, we have to pick up our boots and begin marching forward again.

Life WILL keep going. The question at hand is: Will you keep up or choose to stay stuck in the past?

Week 20, Day 5

Get Inspired:

"Nature does not hurry, yet everything is accomplished."

-Lao Tzu

Get Aligned:

Why do we rush and embrace the concept of "busy". We each only have 24hours in a day, and how we chose to spend that time is what matters.

If something truly matters to us, we should ensure that we are not in a hurry; let it take the time needed to happen. We don't learn to walk overnight, we don't earn our advanced diplomas in one week, we can't build a business in a day, and we don't build meaningful relationships in just one hour.

Nature does not hurry because she knows that time is what makes it special. All that matters will be accomplished if we stay dedicated to it and take our time.

Week 20, Day 6

Get Inspired:

"It's okay to be discouraged. It's not okay to quit."

-Ryan Holiday

Get Aligned:

Disappointment and becoming discouraged are part of life. Quitting in the face of a challenge is a weakness.

If you are discouraged in a situation that you are facing, stop to consider if you are going through a natural cycle of challenge or if you have lost the drive to work towards that goal. Sometimes we need to pivot and adjust our goals. But don't let feelings of frustration or disappointment be the catalyst to pivot. If you never push back against these feelings, you will never find fulfillment and success in achieving your goals.

When you know your True North, you can take the disappointment and give yourself an appropriate break. And then, you get back up and keep pushing towards your personal summit.

Embracing the mindset that disappointments will come and go, and they can be used as fuel to improve is crucial to Owning Your Journey so that you don't give up and fail to make progress.

As a former avid competitor in show jumping of horses, I faced plenty of disappointments. I was highly competitive in both my mind and in reality; therefore, I usually ranked near the top in competitions. In this world of competition when you are asking your horse to jump multiple 4'6" fences at a brisk pace, control and detail are everything. An eighth of a second or a fourth of an inch could mean the difference between 1st place and 4th place. I had some disappointing results at various shows over the years but took those disappointments to use as fuel in my training. With my trainer we would analyze where the tweaks could be made and work diligently to improve for the next round. THIS is the mindset that will carry you through many of life's crazy challenges.

Week 20, Day 7

Reflect:

What inspired you this week?

What will you carry forward?

Week 21, Day 1

Get Inspired:

"Wealth is the ability to fully experience life."

– Henry David Thoreau

Get Aligned:

We often refer to wealth as though money is the only asset of value. In fact, the wealthiest people are not the richest people. They are the ones who find fulfillment and happiness daily.

If you are to truly Own Your Journey, to be a leader of self, you must embrace life and experience it in color. Don't hide behind the "what ifs" and "it feels scary". Take calculated risks, be brave, and embrace life.

Wealthy is a mindset. When we begin to live fully present in our lives and know what we are living for, that is when we will be truly wealthy.

Week 21, Day 2

Get Inspired:

"The only real psychological safety is when you are dead."

-Eric Blondeau

Get Aligned:

Frenchman, Eric Blondeau is an expert at behavioral mechanisms and decision making. He studies and teaches what he describes as the 11 levers of decision making. In his work, he has found that we are always in a bit of turmoil because we are constantly making decisions. Ergo, the belief that true psychological safety only comes when we are dead and no longer able to think.

If this is the case, we should be relieved to hear that as humans are all finding a bit of strife in any thought or decision-making process we face. Embrace the discomfort and continue to align your mindset to reflect your vision.

Go forward knowing that it will be hard, you will feel challenged, and you will likely feel some discomfort. But know that this is universal for all of us, and that you are indeed growing in your self-leadership when you are willing to make choices, to follow your vision, and to cultivate a presence that supports your goals. How easy it would be to simply drift through life with no control over where we want to go, and how incredibly unfulfilling it would be.

Week 21, Day 3

<u>Get Inspired:</u>

"The soul would have no rainbow if the eyes had no tears."

-Native American Proverb

<u>Get Aligned:</u>

Tough times are more than tough. They can feel soul crushing. They can challenge all of our preconceived notions and life beliefs. They make the air feel thick and time stand still.

Yet we must remember, from every dark time there is a lesson learned or a new path revealed.

This doesn't mean that the hurting goes away, it simply means we can lose a branch whilst simultaneously growing a new leaf.

~

When it comes to others, be there. When you see someone around you hurting, be there. Don't judge their grief process or the roller coaster of emotions that accompany it. Allow and encourage them to feel their emotions. Be a spark of love/trust/support in their life which they might desperately need.

As you work to be a great leader of self, embrace the mindset that you can and will work through the hard times. In that process, allow yourself to navigate your grief process in a way that is authentic to your needs.

Week 21, Day 4

<u>Get Inspired:</u>

"The morale is to the physical as 3 to 1."

– Napoleon Bonaparte

<u>Get Aligned:</u>

Napoleon is known for being a small in stature man, but with a huge impact as a leader. This quote gives a solid glimpse into why he was so successful.

When we focus on our mindset and mental focus, it is 3x stronger than our physical attributes. Consider many great athletes over time, not all were destined for great athletic prowess. Numerous athletes have been studied and interviewed to reveal just how important the mental game is to the process of wining the physical game.

The same is true for any endeavor we wish to explore. When we fix our minds on positive actions and outcomes, we can overcome physical limitations such as time, strength, education, experience, and so much more.

Therefore, it is imperative that we practice daily positive affirmations which allow our brains to visualize the positive outcome; to practice daily gratitude so that we can remain in a positive headspace; to practice daily micro-habits which will reinforce to our brains that we are indeed making progress. Own Your Journey by owning your mindset practices.

Week 21, Day 5

Get Inspired:

"The greatest discovery of my generation is that human beings can alter their lives by altering their attitude of mind."

-William James

Get Aligned:

William James was born in the mid-1800s and died in the early 1900s. His forward-thinking ideals as a psychologist put forth that we can control our experiences in life by using the power of altering our mindset to adjust how we perceive events.

Basically, he was telling us that mindset matters. That we can own our mindset and adjust our lives by focusing our minds. We can choose to live in a negative space by staying in a negative mindset, or we can live in a more optimistic space by focusing on opportunities, gratitude, joy, abundance, and other positive mindsets.

He was, in short, challenging us to view the same glass as half-empty or half-full.

The power of his discoveries and theories have given us the permission to choose our mindset and go forth from there to create change in our lives.

Week 21, Day 6

<u>Get Inspired:</u>

"No man will make a great leader who wants to do it all himself or get all the credit for doing it."

-Andrew Carnegie

<u>Get Aligned:</u>

Focusing inward on only yourself, your outcomes, and how you will succeed in life is the opposite of an abundant mindset. You are narrowing your field of view and your field of influence so that you end up in a space of lack.

By embracing abundance, you will see the value in acknowledging others, helping others, and sharing with others. The sheer power of joy and positive energy that comes from these efforts is not only contagious, but it is creating more abundance around you in an exponential fashion.

Every energy carries a ripple effect. Why not choose abundance and extend the energy beyond yourself?

Week 21, Day 7

Reflect:

What inspired you this week?

What will you carry forward?

Week 22, Day 1

Get Inspired:

"Parents can only give good advice or put them on the right paths, but the final forming of a person's character lies in their own hands."

– Anne Frank

Get Aligned:

We have a choice. We can truly be whomever we wish to be in life.

You can go through life blaming your parents, authority figures, and/or bosses for the things that are wrong or unfair in life … or you can decide who you want to be and how you want to live and pursue it.

Yes, some people will have a leg-up and begin with more opportunities, but never let that be an excuse for becoming the person you want to be. Only YOU can be responsible for your character; to challenge how you will show up when things get tough and to keep your mindset curious and positive.

If you want to reach next-level joy/success/harmony/learning/contentment in your life, you must learn to be a great leader of self. And that begins with owning your character and a positive mindset.

Week 22, Day 2

Get Inspired:

"Change how you see and see how you change."

-Zen Proverb

Get Aligned:

This one is so incredibly simple that you may have to read it twice to get it!

If you are failing to challenge your own viewpoints throughout life, you are your own worst enemy. You need not change your views constantly, but you should spot check your strong opinions and listen to the other side. This is where learning takes place and where you may find growth; or you may find a deeper resolve in your current beliefs. Either way, you are being honest with yourself and open-minded to the world of growth.

Week 22, Day 3

Get Inspired:

"You yourself are the eternal energy which appears as this Universe. You didn't come into this world; you came out of it. Like a wave from the ocean."

-Alan Watts

Get Aligned:

If you are part of this Universe, then it makes sense that you can harness the powers of the Universe. You can manage your mindsets and actions to produce a better world around you.

Knowing that you have access to unlimited support and power from the Universe can be a daunting belief for some. Allow yourself to contemplate this concept often as you slowly lean into the abundance at your disposal. Practice embracing this positive mindset daily until it becomes habitual.

A note on Karma:

Use your powers for good. Do not merely think of how you can help yourself in this life, but what you can do to help others. And do this daily; even the tiniest gesture of smiling at a stranger may improve her entire day.

Week 22, Day 4

Get Inspired:

"Acknowledging the good that you already have in your life is the foundation for all abundance."

-Eckhart Tolle

Get Aligned:

If you truly want to live in harmony, you must believe in abundance. Abundance is the notion that enough exists and is already available to you.

By simply acknowledging and thanking the Universe for the abundance that is all around you (health, joy, love, wealth, safety, success, etc.) you are attracting the abundance to you.

It is really that simple! Don't expect the sky to start raining money, but you will find as you continue your practice of belief in abundance, that you will find it all around you on a more frequent basis.

Try this daily mantra as you get started:

"Abundance flows to me easily and freely; I embody abundance."

~

Why not spread abundance by taking a moment to thank the Universe for bestowing it on someone else in your life? Boosting them does not mean less for you; by its definition, abundance means there is enough for everyone.

Week 22, Day 5

Get Inspired:

"Because when you stop and look around, this life is pretty amazing."

-Dr. Suess

Get Aligned:

Joy is everywhere to be found. You need only look for it.

If you are having a bad day, that is the time to intentionally open your eyes and look for the amazing things all around you.

If you find you are in a slump, keep a Joy Journal. It can be photos, writings, positive posts on social media, or even doodles that capture small moments of joy for yourself each day. As you continue to build the collection, you will look back and be overwhelmed by the amount of joy you encounter daily.

~

As you seek to build a positive mindset which will feed into your Own Journey, take time to look for the amazement around you each day.

Week 22, Day 6

<u>Get Inspired:</u>

Dominant brain waves change throughout your day based upon the activity at hand. *Delta* waves are in force when we sleep, *Gamma* waves are at their peak when we are super relaxed (interestingly enough, during this time the brain is exploding with ideas), *Theta* waves rule when we are in deep creativity mode, *Alpha* waves support a relaxed state, and *Beta* waves are superior for our deep thinking.

<u>Get Aligned:</u>

Notice how you feel when you are striving for different tasks. If it feels forced, your brain may not be on the same wavelength as you. Apply these situational tips to help achieve the desired state:

Delta: Invite sleep by preparing a quiet dark space without bluescreens.

Gamma: Take a walk outdoors without distractions or a drive through the countryside, have a notepad and pen nearby to capture your thoughts as they begin to explode in your brain.

Theta: Making time for meditation or a long hot shower will help to get you here.

Alpha: Go ahead and finish that lingering project, you will naturally find Alpha at the completion.

Beta: Prepare a quiet and uninterrupted space for deep thought; turnoff digital distractions, use noise cancelling headphones or stream classical music, put away clutter and to-do lists.

Make these practices habitual to reduce the friction produced when trying to enter each state. You are the keeper of your mindset.

Week 22, Day 7

Reflect:

What inspired you this week?

What will you carry forward?

Week 23, Day 1

Get Inspired:

Quantum Theory (also known as quantum physics) is the foundational basis for present-day material science. The theory explains the nature and behavior of matter and energy on the atomic level and is useful in understanding our own presence in the world. Quantum physics teaches that nothing is fixed, that there are no limitations, and that everything is vibrating Energy.

With that understanding, we can attract positive Energy into our lives by focusing on positive and abundant thoughts with the *Law of Attraction*.

In its simplest form, the Law of Attraction states: "Like attracts like".

Get Aligned:

When you practice generating positive, abundant, or productive thoughts, you will attract those things because you are resonating with the same Energy. If you allow yourself to think of the negatives or things you want to avoid, you will inadvertently attract those very things.

Begin by making a simple statement of what you wish to attract (health, safety, a promotion, a wonderful relationship, calm energy, etc.). Repeat this several times each day. It's helpful to have it posted on a piece of paper near your mirror, computer, or in the car ... this makes seeing & saying it easier to remember! If you catch yourself thinking in the negative space, immediately stop and replace that statement with your positive attraction statement. This takes time and practice, but you will find that as you keep going it becomes more natural to lean into the positive and to shut out the negative.

Not sure you believe in this concept? That's ok! I encourage you to try it for a month and see if it changes anything in your life. You have nothing to lose and might just find the power in it along the way!

Week 23, Day 2

Get Inspired:

"Your faith must be fierce, fiery, and not fuckin' around."

-Jen Sincero

Get Aligned:

When you are brave enough to announce to yourself and the Universe what you want to do or achieve in life, you are ready to make some progress!

You must be clear on your intentions, you must embrace the vision, and you must execute by making choices based upon that vision.

When you show up fully like this, there is no limit to what you can do.

This powerful mindset is the fuel to your efforts. This ability to forge a fierce and fiery mindset will propel you along Your Own Journey.

Week 23, Day 3

Get Inspired:

"Those who dwell among the beauties and mysteries of the earth are never alone or weary in life."

-Rachel Carson

Get Aligned:

Be careful not to use and abuse this earth. Instead, lean into her bounty and work with the gifts she offers. When you find a rhythm alongside of nature as opposed to fighting nature, you will find a deeper peace than you knew possible.

When we put good into the world, we receive good back. Do something small each day that is a positive gesture for the earth. In your life planning, be aware of your natural resources and take care to embrace them as part of your path.

Adjust your mindset to be aware and respectful of our earth. A good leader of self does not take resources for granted and uses them wisely along their journey.

Week 23, Day 4

Get Inspired:

"There's only one rule you need to remember: laugh at everything and forget everybody else! It sounds egotistical, but it's actually the only cure for those suffering from self-pity."

– Anne Frank

Get Aligned:

Laughter really is the best medicine. When we learn to laugh at the challenges and mistakes in our lives, we free ourselves from being laughed at.

Others can only shame us if we give them the power to do so. Move from a space of being a victim to a space of owning your reality. Choose to pull an Elsa and *"Let It Go"* … It may feel awkward and unnatural, but it works.

You might be thinking, OK, but how??

Here is a personal example:

I used to worry that others would think I looked foolish trying new things. As a teenager I would never actually dance at dances, for fear of looking stupid. I missed out on a lot of fun because of this fear.

As an adult, I dance at every wedding I attend. I dance around the pool when I like a song, and I definitely dance in my car (much to my tweenager daughter's disapproval. I am dedicated to looking foolish so that I can teach her this exact lesson!).

But I no longer care if I look foolish. That is because one day I finally realized that most other people look foolish, too, when dancing … but they also looked happy! And I was ready to embrace that freedom and happiness.

Nowadays, I go out of my way to do things that make me feel a little bit silly/uncomfortable so that I keep that skill set up. I post videos for work on a regular basis, and sometimes I do so without doing my hair or makeup (which as a woman can be totally intimidating). Admittedly, I still need to hit "post" before I can overthink it and pull back, but I never regret it. I share my thoughts and opinions, even if they may not be mainstream. This book is a great example of putting myself out there. I had an idea; I worried others may not see the value or hard work that goes into it … but decided to push forward and just do it.

A mindset that allows you to 'just do it' without fear of rejection or failure is crucial to your ability to Own Your Journey. If you remain beholden to other's opinions, you will never be free to pursue your journey with passion.

Week 23, Day 5

Get Inspired:

"Joy does not simply happen to us. We have to choose joy and keep choosing it every day."

-Henri Nouwen

Get Aligned:

Do you know those people who always seem happy? Are you jealous of them? Here's a secret, you can be that person, too.

Everyone faces adversity of some type at some point. It's how we hold our *perceptions* of life through these adversities that will influence if we are living in joy or sorrow. If we train our brains to look for the positive, we won't find as many low points in life.

Sadness, sorrow, and loneliness can and will likely show up at some point. If you have been in the practice of finding and banking joy in your life, you will have reserves like a solar battery to help you through the darker times.

Seek joy and invite into your life daily. Focus on the little things; I'm not asking you to be joyful in the face of tragic loss … but don't let small stuff drag you down.

As you find joy, celebrate it. Thank the Universe for it. And share it with others.

Week 23, Day 6

Get Inspired:

"Joy is the feeling we have from doing what we are fashioned to do, no matter the outcome."

-Matthew McConaughey

Get Aligned:

Joy is a mindset or state of being. Happiness is a reaction to a situation or stimulus.

Joy stays with us. Happiness comes and goes.

We can choose to live in joy. Happiness chooses to sometimes grace us with her presence.

~

Personal Checkpoint:

Are you searching for happiness, or choosing to live in joy?

Make the choice now to invest in a lifetime of joy by pursing that which lights you up. Along the way, don't be afraid to embrace happiness in the moments that it finds to you.

If you live in alignment each day with the values, focus, and principles that matter to you … you will live in joy and radiate that energy to others.

Week 23, Day 7

Reflect:

What inspired you this week?

What will you carry forward?

Week 24, Day 1

Get Inspired:

"Celebration is my attitude, unconditional to what life brings."

-Osho

Get Aligned:

What an invigorating way to float through life … by living in a perpetual space of celebration for all that is around you.

Why are we not all embracing this mindset every day? Afterall, life IS a gift.

What will you celebrate today?

Week 24, Day 2

Get Inspired:

"Listen to the mustn'ts, child. Listen to the don'ts. Listen to the shouldn'ts, the impossibles, the won'ts. Listen to the never haves, then listen close to me... Anything can happen, child. Anything can be."
— **Shel Silverstein**

Get Aligned:

I don't know about you, but Shel always seems to hit the nail on the head! His creatively twisting lyrics always make perfect sense when you analyze the message. My 1st grade teacher was a huge fan of Shel Silverstein, and we studied his poems all year long. I can still visualize the oversized posters hanging in his classroom with images and lyrics from popular poems. To this day, I can still recite most of "A Polar Bear in the Frigidaire".

Mr. Silverstein is the perfect example of creativity and a positive mindset swirled together to inspire us. When we listen to the nay-sayers but then choose to pursue the "what may be", we are doubling down on the strength of self-leadership. We are taking in information and filtering out the "lack mindset". We are stepping up to the plate (even if we are afraid) and remain curious to see what we can do.

If you are struggling with a limited or lack mindset, I encourage you to pick up one of Shel's classics and inspire yourself for what could be! Leaning into the belief of abundance and opportunity is crucial for maintaining a strong sense of self-leadership. As leaders of self, we cannot rely on others to lift us up, point us in the right direction, or tell us where to go. We must dig deep, trust our instincts, be willing to try and fail, and to go forth with our own plans.

Week 24, Day 3

Get Inspired:

"When one door of happiness closes, another opens; but often we look so long at the closed door that we do not see the one which has been opened for us."
— Helen Keller

Get Aligned:

This is one of the most difficult lessons in self-leadership and mindset. Allowing yourself to see the possibilities beyond the door that has closed / the opportunity lost. It is human nature to fixate on what has been lost or taken from us. However, if we can reframe our thinking to see this as a marker pointing us in a new direction, we gain freedom from that perceived loss and can use our energies in pursuing a new opportunity.

There is a finite amount of energy that we can exert each day, through our thoughts and actions combined. If we use that resource worrying or mourning the closed door, we are wasting energy that could be put to more productive use exploring what comes next.

Example: I was courting a very high-profile corporate client, one who was on my dream list of partnerships. I had a wonderful contact who was eager and excited about what I could do for them. We spent 6 months talking and planning; I prepared an in-depth custom proposal for this multi-year project. It had gone through many layers of approvals, and we were waiting for the final "blessing" from the powers that be.

Unfortunately, the top decision maker said NO because they had another pilot happening abroad which was similar to my program.

I was devastated. I had spent more hours and brain power than I care to share and was excited for the possibilities of the impact I would make.

The door slammed shut in my face. I wanted to cry, to be angry, to "fix it". But there was nothing to be done. It was a blow to my ego, my energy, and my vision. I had to dig really deep to find the open window; it felt like weeks of wandering through the dark hallway of disappointment.

Finally, it came to me. This exercise was an incredible learning experience, AND it allowed me to design a new cutting-edge program that I otherwise may not have prioritized. It gave me deep insights into companies of this size and complexity so that I could be better prepared to offer above average solutions to future prospects.

It was a window to the future.

Don't fear the closed door, keep moving until you find that next window and look through it to see what possibilities lie ahead!

Week 24, Day 4

Get Inspired:

"We are never more fully alive, more completely ourselves, or more deeply engrossed in anything, than when we are at play."

– Charles Schaefer

Get Aligned:

Owning Your Journey largely means being willing to embrace joy along the way, despite the setbacks, curve balls, and challenges. It means that we refuse to let the tough circumstances own us, rather, we choose to move forward with a positive outlook. It is a mindset focused on opportunity.

When we play, we are at our best because we are embracing joy on a deeper level without scrutinizing the why/when/how of the situation. When we play, we free our minds to bathe in joy as we let our guard down. This in turn fuels our inner fire, our self-confidence, and stamina for life. Play trains our mindset to be open, fun, and curious.

~

I am fortunate enough to have a small group of women with whom I occasionally get to ride horses. When our schedules do align and we get together, the time is spent with laughter and play. We let go of the "goals" and "training agenda" to simply enjoy the time with each other on our equine friends. It always reminds me of my youth, of the friendships forged and lessons learned on horseback. This time for play always puts a smile on my face and sets my mood up to be productive and resilient in the afterglow of play.

When was the last time you played? Maybe you are overdue.

Week 24, Day 5

Get Inspired:

"One way to get the most out of life is to look upon it as an adventure."

– William Feather

Get Aligned:

Life does not OWE us anything. We are here, and we all face different challenges.

To approach life as an adventure in which we face new challenges will help to keep the pressures from becoming too heavy.

For example, when my family took our first trip post-COVID we went to Jamaica. The resort we booked was a disaster. Disgusting rooms, terrible food, moldy pools, stinky pool decks, all of it. Our first inclination was to freak out ... and that we did for a little it. Soon, however, we put aside the disappointment of where we were and instead planned our transfer to a new resort. Once settled in appropriate lodging, we found endless entertainment in the story! We had to look at the situation and laugh or else be consumed by the frustration.

The choice is ours to make. Your mindset is your reality.

Week 24, Day 6

<u>Get Inspired:</u>

"Technique and ability alone do not get you to the top; it is the willpower that is most important."

– Junko Tabei

<u>Get Aligned:</u>

Junko Tabei was a Japanese mountaineer, and the first woman to summit Mount Everest. Knowing this, it may surprise you to learn that growing up she was considered a very frail child; but she began climbing anyway. As she pursued a career in the then male-dominated sport of climbing. Although she was not always welcomed by the majority, she persisted. At the age of 73 she was diagnosed with stomach cancer; yet she continued climbing mountains, including leading a youth expedition up Mount Fuji in the year of her death.

She has shown by example over and over throughout her life how being the favored, the strongest, or most skilled is not enough to get you to the top. Her strength of drive and willpower is what took her to heights that most humans will never reach. She was facing mountains in both the figurative and literal sense, and she stayed with her willpower to achieve.

When we are determined to Own Our Journey, we simply need to be clear on what we want to achieve, set out a plan to get the skills and support needed for the journey, and to keep going even when things are tough. That is the only true way to achieve your goals. Willpower cannot be manufactured to simply please others. If we are not clearly aligned with our goals or if we are pursuing someone else's goals, our willpower will never be strong enough to get us there.

Week 24, Day 7

<u>Reflect:</u>

What inspired you this week?

What will you carry forward?

Week 25, Day 1

<u>Get Inspired:</u>

"When the debate is lost, slander becomes the tool of the loser."

-Socrates

<u>Get Aligned:</u>

Don't be bitter.

Possibly one of the most profound lessons in life as we navigate our Own Journey; bitterness pulls us into the abyss of lack and depression. We begin to focus on what others have, and what we lack. Jealousy builds and clouds our logical judgement.

If you have accidentally stepped onto the bitter-train, do everything in your power to jump off! Double down on positive journaling, gratitude statements, creative endeavors, complimenting others, prayer, positive affirmations, therapy, or play time. Any of these can have a positive shifting effect on your energy.

You are in control of your mind, don't give that power away to a wasteful force such as bitterness.

Week 25, Day 2

Get Inspired:

"You are responsible for your life. You can't keep blaming somebody else for your dysfunction. Life is really about moving on."

-Oprah Winfrey

Get Aligned:

There are people who dwell on the past or on what others have "done to them". And then there are people who acknowledge the bumps but more forward.

Don't become the person who gets stuck in the blame game. You will probably have supporters when you begin the blaming. But soon those around you will grow tired of the charade and move on. You will be stuck wasting precious time and energy thinking about how someone else is responsible for your situation.

Let's be real here ... we ALL have some sort of dysfunctional operating system onboard. Embrace it, work on it, and keep forward focused. Develop the self-responsible mindset that a true leader of self carries, and you will go far in life.

~

Imagine your life as a labyrinth; the type where you must try many paths to find your way forward. Each time you hit a dead-end, pivot and return to a fresh intersection. Mark your mistakes along the way so that you don't repeat them. Stay focused on the forward momentum.

Week 25, Day 3

Get Inspired:

"Every negative is a positive. The bad things that happen to me, I somehow make them good. That means you can't do anything to hurt me."

-Curtis James Jackson, III; aka: 50Cent

Get Aligned:

50Cent grew up in some of the most dangerous and challenging spaces that we can image. And yet, he refused to be a victim. He refused to be scared. He refused to let fear win or cloud his forward-thinking plans for success.

Having the capacity to look at the negatives in life and finding a way to turn them into positives may not be easy but it is available to each of us. Each negative encounter teaches us a lesson and gives us leverage for the next time that we encounter a challenge.

If we cultivate the mindset that we can make lemonade out of any lemon, then we cannot become a victim of circumstance. The challenges then become not roadblocks, but detours which may take a scenic route we did not expect. Cling to your personal compass, keep your eyes open for the lesson, find the silver lining and carry it forward with you. Never get bogged down in the perceived roadblock. Rough terrain is a challenge, but often offers the most inspiring views.

To Own Your Journey, you must first own your mindset.

~

The story of rapper 50Cent rising from the streets as a young drug-dealer into a self-made businessman is incredible. He has faced challenges that most of us will never know. Be sure to read his story for more inspiration on creating your own path in life.

Week 25, Day 4

Get Inspired:

"I would rather die of passion than of boredom."

-Vincent Van Gogh

Get Aligned:

Anyone can come up with a vision that they believe in or want to bring to life. Establishing a mindset around that vision is the fuel that will bring your vision to life in the end. Our passion is what helps to share our mindset, and our mindset in turn can support or degrade our passion.

Mastering the art of maintaining a productive and positive mindset is key to your success as a good leader of self.

Our mindset should be steeped in gratitude for all that is good around us, should always consider each action we plan to take with a positive intent, and should build confidence in ourselves. We must learn to have patience, as some of our visions will take years, decades, or lifetimes to realize. In the end, what matters is *not* the destination; real living is about the art of *navigating* our Own Journey.

Week 25, Day 5

Get Inspired:

"Where the head goes, the body follows. Perception precedes action. Right action follows the right perspective."

-Ryan Holiday

Get Aligned:

Our minds hold incredible power over us. We can convince ourselves to do all sorts of difficult things, by merely believing that we can.

To improve our abilities as a leader of self, we therefore must improve our mindset. Practicing intentional thoughts that support our morals, our goals, and our dreams for the future will have a direct impact on the actions that we take.

When we spend time thinking about the how, the why, and the positive possibilities we are preparing our bodies for productive action.

Conversely, we will always struggle to meet our goals if we live in a headspace of negativity, "I can't", fear, and doubt.

Positive mantras and daily affirmation statements are wonderful tools to achieve the positive mental space required to prepare your body for the proper actions and habits which support your goals. Think of a sentence or two that captures the essence, success, and positive energy surrounding a goal that you have. Hang onto that sentence and repeat it daily.

Week 25, Day 6

Get Inspired:

"Your body hears everything your mind says."

-Naomi Judd

Get Aligned:

Do you whisper or yell at yourself? Do you encourage or admonish yourself?

How are those results working out for you?

If you truly want to be a good leader of self, then start *acting* like a good leader. A good leader is one that draws out the best from those that follow, not someone who leads through fear and negativity.

A great leader of self (or others) will challenge the status quo with encouragement, will create inspiration for what can be, will hold yourself accountable for efforts not made, will pivot when you reach a dead-end, will see and believe in your vision, and will acknowledge the progress as it comes.

A good leader holds the vision for their followers, and keeps them focused on what they can do, how they can do it, and how to keep going. Doing this for yourself will equip you with a lifetime of possibilities and support the process of Owning Your Journey.

Week 25, Day 7

Reflect:

What inspired you this week?

What will you carry forward?

Week 26, Day 1

<u>Get Inspired:</u>

It turns out that men and women really do think differently!

There are two types of brain matter; gray and white matter. Men and women each have both, but at different capacities.

Men have higher levels of gray matter than women do. Gray matter is known for isolated problem solving.

Women have higher levels of white matter than men. White matter plays a crucial role in integrating information.

The impact?

Men often have an easier time digging deep on a single project as opposed to many things at once.

Women on the other hand, have a brain that is almost always more active (which isn't necessarily a good thing). "One study suggests that women have 30% more neurons firing at any given time than men." This means "women can get stuck on certain thoughts or behaviors, such as worrying; but women are also better at multitasking."

-Katty Kay and Claire Shipman, *The Confidence Code*, Harper Collins Publishers, 2014, pg. 111.

<u>Get Aligned:</u>

I could write an entire book on this topic, but I won't because there are many good ones out there that effectively cover the concepts.

The takeaway here is this:

Neither the male nor female brain is superior. They are different, and when we use them together (in business or personal adventures) we can often achieve higher outcomes, IF we know what pitfalls and strengths to look out for in ourselves and our counterparts.

If you are a woman, you CAN focus in on one task … it just might take extra effort.

If you are a man, you CAN connected the random dots to create a clear picture … it may just take a little longer.

Know your superpowers; know your limiting factors. Work to respectively exploit and overcome these innate features. That is where you will find the greatest success.

Understanding your mindset unlocks doors of clarity as you pursue Your Own Journey.

Week 26, Day 2

Get Inspired:

"The mind shapes the body, and the body shapes the mind."

-Amy Cuddy

Get Aligned:

When we think that we cannot do something, we rarely can.

Have you ever been in a fitness class, and you are dog-tired, ready to give up? Then that loud instructor yells "You CAN do this! Don't give up!". And in that moment, you stay the course; you keep peddling or keep curling the dumbbell. Maybe you are a bit slower than you would prefer, and you are huffing and puffing more than usual. But you get it done because someone reminds you that you CAN.

Our mind-body connection is on a constant feedback cycle. One challenges the other, and it responds in kind.

When we tell our body, "Keep going", we do. When our body keeps going, our mind believes we can.

Never have I ever learned this lesson more clearly than when giving birth. I've done it twice, and both times were by far the most challenging physical and mental events that I have ever faced. You are in pain and exhaustion beyond description, and yet you keep going because you know you CAN, and you MUST. Your mind tells your body to push once more, and your body pushes in response … this tells your brain that you are capable; and so, the cycle continues until you bring a new life into the world.

We all have an immense power source within us *if* we take the time to let our brains and bodies talk to each other.

When you feel nervous, give your body a confident stance and your brain will begin to believe you are OK. When you need to be heard, channel a thoughtful voice and your body language will follow. When you need space to rest and recover, be still and your mind will eventually settle. When you want to be empathetic to a friend/child/spouse you are frustrated with, extend a hug to them and your brain will begin to soften its frustrations.

We can shape our mindset. And our mindset does shape our reality.

Week 26, Day 3

Get Inspired:

"One generation plants the tree and the other gets the shade."

-Chinese Proverb

Get Aligned:

In a nutshell, this is telling us: Do good in this world, even if you don't benefit.

This is all about Karma, the grand equalizer in life. When you take your focus away from "what's in it for me", and shift to "how can I make a positive impact", the reward will flow to you.

This sentiment applies heavily to networking as well! Many people are leery of networking because it feels "fake". The truth is, if you go into the process wanting to truly KNOW people, and to be open to HELPING people along their path … you WILL find it fulfilling and empowering.

Putting your needs first can become a reflex. Try to break the auto-habit by choosing one thing each day that you can do for someone else and expect nothing in return. That means, don't get upset if you don't receive a "Thank You" or even an acknowledgement of your efforts. It must be purely for the effort of helping a fellow human, a community, an animal, or our planet.

Week 26, Day 4

Get Inspired:

"A lot of voices are clamoring out there for your attention. As you think about how to spend your listening time, keep in mind that you have two purposes for listening: to connect with people and to learn."

-John C. Maxwell, *21 Indispensable Qualities of a Leader*, Thomas Nelson Publishers, 1999, pg.77

Get Aligned:

Learning to listen is a key portion in the equation of communication and connection. However, what you listen to is critical to your ability as a leader of self. What we listen to and how we receive it impacts our mindset.

These guidelines from John Maxwell regarding the purpose of listening are genius. If the time we spend listening does not either connect you with someone or help you to learn anything, then what have you accomplished?

As you proceed through your day and take in the various voices, continue to filter as you go, asking yourself if you are either connecting or learning. When talking with your team at work, you are likely doing it right if you are achieving both connection and learning. The same applies to engaging with your children or personal relationships. We want to connect to the people around us, and learn more about their ideas, their passions, and their challenges.

When listening to books, podcasts, videos, or TV, you are more likely learning than connecting; and we should all make time for that. *Sidebar-* A fun exercise in growth involves listening to a program that shares an opposite opinion of your own. Use that time to truly try and learn from the other party. Why do they feel this way? Why does this not settle with you? What can you learn from their differing opinions?

Attending a networking event? What a great opportunity to connect with people that you don't already know. Seek to hear their story, their strengths, and their passions. Look for areas of overlap where you can connect on a deeper level.

It is worth noting, we are not robots. There will be times when we listen for pure entertainment, and that is ok! I would caution that if most of your listening time is spent *only* on entertainment, it may be time to adjust how you spend your time. Likewise, if you find that you are *never* listening for entertainment, try to loosen up and allow yourself some downtime on a regular basis.

Listening to a variety of content and people will help to expand your mindset into a space of more reflective thought.

Week 26, Day 5

<u>Get Inspired:</u>

"Nobody with a victim mentality will get anywhere, ever. They will never succeed."

-Jon Lovitz

<u>Get Aligned:</u>

Nothing is more damaging than believing you *cannot* because of someone else. Why would you give away your power like that?

In my line of work, I witness many people who *say* that they want change, and yet continuously find excuses to avoid change. They blame everyone around them for change not happening, expect themselves. They work overtime to find a reason that each solution won't work for them. They are indeed their own biggest obstacle.

Take a moment to be brutally honest with yourself. Do you blame others for your challenges? If you do, it will be very difficult to be a leader to anyone, including yourself. If you blame others, you are often unable to take action to improve your situation, and so the cycle will continue for you.

Be strong enough to take ownership of your life. The outside forces are what they are, we cannot change that. But you CAN decide how you show up, what choices you make, and put forth a great effort despite the challenges that face you. When you fix your mindset to a determined and curious state, it will take you places!

Week 26, Day 6

Get Inspired:

"Happiness is not something ready-made. It comes from your own actions."

-Dalai Lama

Get Aligned:

So much pressure and talk surrounds the concept of "being happy". Happiness is not something that others get or that we lack. It is available to each of us, through our actions. Happiness is a reaction to an action or situation. If you desire the feeling of "happiness", simply do something that inspires a good feeling deep within.

Easy ways to get started?

Read a funny book or watch a funny movie. Journal about the good things in your life. Sing a song. Pick flowers. Take a hike. Take a nap. Pet a dog or cat. Play a sport. Learn a foreign language.

Tiny actions and choices throughout your life string together to give you blips of happiness on your radar. When infused into your life in small quantities on a regular basis, you will feel the continuous loop of happiness that doesn't require someone else to fill the void in your life! And it will help to carry you through the hard times.

Want to feel even happier? Do a good deed for others, it boosts your happy quotient!

Hold the door for a stranger. Make eye contact with someone and compliment them. Deliver a card or flowers to someone you love for no reason at all. Bake cookies for a neighbor. Make mudpies with your kids. Volunteer within a community group.

Choose to remain in a positive mindset by creating space for happiness to thrive.

Week 26, Day 7

<u>Reflect:</u>

What inspired you this week?

What will you carry forward?

Week 27, Day 1

Get Inspired:

Science writer **Winifred Gallagher** discovered a strong connection between attention and happiness after a difficult cancer diagnosis.

She stated that *"Diverse disciplines from anthropology to education, behavioral economics to family counseling, similarly suggest that the **skillful management of attention** is the sine qua non of the good life and the **key to improving virtually every aspect of your experience**."*

Get Aligned:

Staying focused on the positive is the key to happiness.

Therefore, why do we wallow in dread, the uncertain, the scary, and the doubt? We are the masters of our mind, yet we often turn our thoughts over to outside forces.

Begin by noticing your negative thoughts. Take action by redirecting your thoughts to positive spaces. Encourage this habit by providing visual cues for your brain, a positive quote, sticky note, or image hung in a prominent place to remind you of your power to invoke happy thoughts.

Own your mindset: manage your attention to the positive, the important, and the possible.

Week 27, Day 2

Get Inspired:

"If you desire to be an effective leader, having a positive attitude is essential. It not only determines your level of contentment as a person, but it also has an impact on how others interact with you. To learn more about what it means to be positive, think on these things:

Your attitude is a choice … Your attitude determines your actions … Your people are a mirror of your attitude … Maintaining a good attitude is easier than regaining one."

-John C. Maxwell, *21 Indispensable Qualities of a Leader*, Thomas Nelson Publishers, 1999, pg.90-92.

Get Aligned:

I like to think of attitude and mindset in comparison to our physical care and activity. People don't stay active by accident. Nor do people stay in a positive mindset by accident. Both are a daily choice and commitment through your actions to live in the space that you desire.

If you doubt your ability to do this, consider it from this angle:

Your attitude is your choice; scheduling time each day to walk or move your body is your choice.

Your attitude determines your actions; your commitment to stay active propels you to avoid a sedentary lifestyle.

Your people are a mirror of your attitude; your vitals reflect the attention you give to maintaining your health.

Maintaining a good attitude is easier than regaining one; committing to light-moderate activity daily is much easier than trying to "get in shape" after months of not using your body.

You don't need to be the most bubbly or effervescent person in the room, and you don't need to train for a triathlon. You merely need to remind yourself to look for the positive in every day, and to use your body in some capacity each day.

Training your brain for a positive mindset is a daily commitment if you wish to Own Your Journey.

Week 27, Day 3

Get Inspired:

"There is no limit to the amount of good you can do if you don't care who gets the credit."

– Ronald Regan

Get Aligned:

When we begin from a place of positive intent, there is no limit to what you can achieve.

When you take the selfish notion out of the work you do, and instead focus on the good that it is providing for others, you will find the load easier to carry. As a parent, when you focus on raising kind, well-adjusted, and productive members of society it can ease the strain of the overwhelming responsibility and challenges of parenthood.

Practice shining a light on others who support you in positive causes or work. Lifting others up does not force you down; often they will grab your hand and pull you up with them!

The amount of joy that is planted in your heart when you do a good deed for others can grow a vast forest of goodness. Try to do an anonymous good deed for someone else on a regular basis and see how it impacts you.

Week 27, Day 4

Get Inspired:

"For every minute you are angry you lose sixty seconds of happiness."

— Ralph Waldo Emerson

Get Aligned:

Emotions are powerful and sometimes catch us off guard. We should always strive to remember that emotions are simply chemical messengers who are asking us to react; they want us to recognize a bad or good situation and react accordingly.

But this doesn't mean that we must overreact and let our emotions get the best of us. Letting go of anger is a powerful tool of self-leadership, and one that can be difficult to embrace. Sometimes we latch onto that anger because it feels real. But again, it is simply a passing emotion.

The better approach to being a good leader of self is to acknowledge the anger, ask yourself why you are angry, and what you can achieve by hanging onto that anger. At that moment, when you realize there is nothing to be gained by remaining angry, you are free to divert your attention elsewhere.

Think of or do something that makes you happy, do a good deed for someone else, or simply pause to say a statement of gratitude. Each of these will rewire your brain into a more positive space and unconsciously start sending happiness hormones to replace the angry ones.

Week 27, Day 5

<u>Get Inspired:</u>

"Folks are usually about as happy as they make their minds
up to be."
— Abraham Lincoln

<u>Get Aligned:</u>

Wise old Abe knew what he was talking about, long before
mindset training became a "thing". Yes, mindset training.

Our minds have fantastic control over our moods, our
achievements, our happiness, our physical wellbeing, and our
mental wellbeing. And we have the ultimate control over our
minds!

Does this mean that it is EASY to always keep your mind in a
positive place? No.

But it does mean we each can train our minds to stay in a
place of Happy more often than not. Of course, we will have
real challenges, sadness, fear, and disappointment in life.
These emotions balance out the good times. However, we can
align our minds into a positive talk-track and boost the
amount of Happy that we experience. When we do this, we
have a positive ripple effect on everyone around us. Emotions
and moods are usually highly contagious; fearful, happy,
frantic, depressed, sad, and many others are palpable feelings
that we absorb from others.

When you find yourself slipping into an unnecessary slump of
frustration or disappointment, set your mind on the things

that are good in life. Make those gratitude statements when you are at your lowest point and watch how they help to elevate your mood by a small percentage.

When done on a regular basis, you will train your brain to turn negative thoughts and feelings into possibilities.

Week 27, Day 6

Get Inspired:

"The Universe responds to details. The Universe responds to energy. The Universe responds to badasses."

— Jen Sincero

Get Aligned:

Your energy drives your mindset, and your mindset drives your energy. It is a cyclical symbiotic relationship.

When these two are out of balance, you are a mess. You may SAY that you want to get healthy, yet you keep buying and eating junk food. Or maybe you SAY that you want to start your own business, but you never put any time into research or other positive steps forward.

If you have ever found yourself out-of-balance between your energy and your mindset (and let's face it, we ALL have at times) … it is time for a personal scan.

Take a hard look at yourself. What intentions are you verbalizing, and do they match your mindset AND the energy that you put forth towards these intentions?

Be honest with yourself and do the work to shift your mindset and your energy into deeper alignment. You will continue to spin on the wheel of purgatory until you crash.

It's time to step up and BE a badass!

Week 27, Day 7

Reflect:

What inspired you this week?

What will you carry forward?

Week 28, Day 1

Get Inspired:

"Splendid Truths of Happiness" by Gretchen Rubin

To learn more, please read "The Happiness Project" by Gretchen Rubin.

The First Splendid Truth:

"To be happier, you have to think about feeling good, feeling bad, and feeling right, in an atmosphere of growth."

Get Aligned:

We are going to spend a few days going through the *8 Splendid Truths of Happiness* by Gretchen Rubin, because we should be living a life that is filled with happiness! That doesn't require us to be happy all the time (that is unrealistic), but as a good leader of self, being happy is a marker of how we are doing at this thing called Life.

To begin: Mindset matters.

What we think, we become. If we allow ourselves to believe that we can and should be happy, we will. If we accept that feeling both good and bad are part of the flow of life, the peaks and valleys will be less shocking. When we adopt a growth mindset, one in which we expect both good and bad times as we learn, we will still find happiness in the process of growing.

Week 28, Day 2

Get Inspired:

"Splendid Truths of Happiness" by Gretchen Rubin

To learn more, please read "The Happiness Project" by Gretchen Rubin.

The Second Splendid Truth:

"One of the best ways to make yourself happy is to make other people happy. One of the best ways to make other people happy is to be happy yourself."

Get Aligned:

Mood is contagious.

If I have a grumpy child at home, I am pretty good about pushing through to maintain a happy demeanor... until I'm not. At some point, if they are rooted in their determination to be grumpy, it eventually wears off on me and I find myself also in a sour space.

At times, it becomes a testament of wills to see who will bend first. On the good days, I am able to cajole a grumpy one into a playful mood; on the not so good days I end up joining the sour-puss bench.

The same can be said for offices. Have you ever been an employee facing a merger or buy-out, and the gossip mill begins? People fall into two camps: they are either excited about having a "bigger and better" company purchase the current one, or they are firmly seated on the fear and loathing bus. The ones steeped in fear can spread their energy like wildfire! Leaders know those negative voices are toxic to the organization, and you will soon see people jumping ship if the talk continues for any length of time.

Thankfully, when you spread positive energy, it is ALSO contagious! My favorite example of this is watching a child on the ball field who is less talented than their peers ... and then they make an important play. You start to see the other children go WILD with excitement for this normally unathletic kid, and it is heartwarming.

If you are having an "unhappy" moment or day, extend a gesture of happiness to someone else (even if you have to fake it). A few easy examples include holding the door for and making eye contact with a stranger; complimenting someone on how nice they look today; congratulating a colleague/teammate for a small but notable contribution; or making cookies to share with your family or friends.

As you extend the olive branch of happiness, it inevitably reverberates back to you.

Week 28, Day 3

Get Inspired:

"Splendid Truths of Happiness" by Gretchen Rubin

To learn more, please read "The Happiness Project" by Gretchen Rubin.

The Third Splendid Truth:

"The days are long, but the years are short."

Get Aligned:

Never will anyone know this truth so well as a new parent who brings home that brand-new baby from the hospital. Every hour can seem like *eternity* when they won't sleep or stop crying, and yet they are growing and changing at an astonishing pace that you can't understand where the time has gone!

I distinctly remember one long night the first time we traveled with our new baby girl. If we attempted to lay her down, she would start wailing at the top of her lungs. We were guests at a family member's house, and they had to be up for work early the next morning. And so, I held my baby as I swayed and walked my way around the tiny guest room from 11pm until 6am. I thought I would break from exhaustion. And then, in the blink of an eye she had learned to travel and sleep through the night and one day stopped wanting me to rock or hold her anymore.

When we are in the grind of growth or change, it can feel like a tedious and grueling pace. But the passage of a year often goes without us noticing. We must, therefore, embrace the now in all of its mess, while simultaneously looking to the future and what we are striving for. Let's find the fun and happy moments in the busy pace of life we are in and take the time to reflect and recall the best moments.

The universal truth in the concept of time is this: time passes, and rarely at a pace we prefer. Therefore, we must never take it for granted.

Week 28, Day 4

Get Inspired:

"Splendid Truths of Happiness" by Gretchen Rubin

To learn more, please read "The Happiness Project" by Gretchen Rubin.

The Fourth Splendid Truth:

"You're not happy unless you think you're happy."

Get Aligned:

There has been a great deal of research on the topic of happiness, especially in the wake of the COVID-19 pandemic. In Gretchen Rubin's book, "The Happiness Project", she shares that "According to current research, in the determination of a person's level of happiness" is related to:

Genetics = 50%

Life Circumstances = 10-20%

How a Person Thinks and Acts = 30-40%

This indicates that 1/3 or greater of the ability to be happy hinges on how we think and act. When we take time to recall what we are grateful for, what is going well in our lives, and what we are happy about … we are increasing our happiness ability by training our brains to think in a positive manner.

Once again, we are reminded of the power of our mindset to shape our reality!

Week 28, Day 5

Get Inspired:

"Splendid Truths of Happiness" by Gretchen Rubin

To learn more, please read "The Happiness Project" by Gretchen Rubin.

The Fifth Splendid Truth:

"I can build a happy life only on the foundation of my own nature."

Get Aligned:

Know yourself and your True North.

We will never find true happiness if we are following along someone else's path, especially if it doesn't resonate with our own True North.

The first step of self-leadership is having awareness of self and what we value. We must take the time to know what OUR dreams and goals are, not just default to what others expect of us. This awareness allows us to funnel our efforts clearly in alignment with our goals so that we can achieve at higher levels.

The process of knowing your true North is what builds a happy life. You are laying one brick at a time, slowly over the years, in pursuit of a blueprint that is beautiful to YOU.

If you want to Own Your Journey, you cannot skip this most basic and often ignored step of the process … be true to yourself and your visions.

Week 28, Day 6

<u>Get Inspired:</u>

"Splendid Truths of Happiness" by Gretchen Rubin

To learn more, please read "The Happiness Project" by Gretchen Rubin.

The Sixth Splendid Truth:

"The only person I can change is myself."

<u>Get Aligned:</u>

Spend your energy on that which you can control.

When is the last time that you got worked up about something, only to finally admit to yourself that you didn't have any control over the situation?

My coaching client, "Mandy", was facing a restructuring where she worked. Her assigned manager was in limbo, and she was forced into that uncomfortable space of waiting to find out what was happening next, and who would be leading her team. She was anxious about where she would be placed, and who she would be reporting to. The firm shared the pending news, and then waited for months to outline the actual structure.

Mandy had a choice, stress over what was to come (knowing that she had absolutely zero control of the outcome), or move forward with planning her future. She is a wise woman, and so she decided to lean into planning her future. She began proactively job searching and interviewing with companies. It had been >8 years since she last interviewed, and she knew this might be a good time to see what else was out there in the world. Additionally, she started thinking about her job responsibilities, her successes, and where she needed more support in her role. Mandy was preparing a mental portfolio to be able to discuss with whomever the new manager was so that she would be prepared to jump right into building that relationship and giving him/her a snapshot of her working history in addition to what her professional goals were. She was also preparing her resume and interviewing skills so that she could make a transition if the new placement turned out to be less than desirable.

By clarifying for herself what she COULD control, this normally stressful time instead became a time of happy exploration for Mandy!

~

Focusing your mind on what you CAN impact is imperative so that you can preserve your energy for efforts worth making.

Week 28, Day 7

Reflect:

What inspired you this week?

What will you carry forward?

Week 29, Day 1

<u>Get Inspired:</u>

"Splendid Truths of Happiness" by Gretchen Rubin

To learn more, please read "The Happiness Project" by Gretchen Rubin.

The Seventh Splendid Truth:

"Happy people make people happy, but I can't make someone be happy and no one else can make me happy."

<u>Get Aligned:</u>

As a leader of yourself, your happiness is your own responsibility.

Give up the notion and heavy baggage of being angry, disappointed, or upset with someone else because they did not fulfill your happiness. That is a lost cause that will always wear down your emotions, leaving you in a negative space.

One of the strongest hallmarks of a good leader of self is the ability to take ownership of our present situation, our future plans, and our individual emotions!

In each situation, look for a reason to be happy. If you can't find it in the present, make specific changes that will allow you to be happy in the future.

Remember that your emotions do not define you; they are merely chemical messengers letting you know that the brain is either happy or unhappy with a situation. Emotions are transient, not a rule of who you are or how to live.

Week 29, Day 2

Get Inspired:

"Splendid Truths of Happiness" by Gretchen Rubin

To learn more, please read "The Happiness Project" by Gretchen Rubin.

The Eighth Splendid Truth:

"Now is now."

Get Aligned:

Be present in the moment, the right here, right now,

How much of your day do you spend worrying about what is to come next, or thinking about what you have already done?

I am a guilty party in this worthless endeavor.

If I feel I have made a mistake or let someone down, it can be hard for me to stop ruminating on it. And as I plan for the future, sometimes I get so wrapped around the axel of 'what is next' that I fail to be present in the moment.

The one thing that keeps us most grounded in the past or the future is our smart phone (or another personal device). It taunts us and pulls at us to put our attention elsewhere. We become subliminally seduced by these electronics without even knowing it.

To overcome these tendencies to "check out" of the current moment, try implementing a few rules. Pick from this list, or create one of your own (after all, this is YOUR journey).

1. Set silent / do not disturb hours on your phone. Mine is from 9pm at night until 7am. This starts 60-90minutes before I go to sleep and doesn't come back to life until after I have been awake for several hours. This buffer zone intentionally lets me step away from the notifications and electronic pull which only serves to disconnect me from my family.

2. Have a block of the day that is "no phone zone". For our family, this is dinner. We aren't always perfect at following it, but we do work to call each other out if the rule is broken! We also have a rule about no devices (for anyone, even children) if we go to a restaurant together.

3. Keep some sort of game or interactive activity close at hand to the place that your family or friends gather. Set restrictions around TV or Video Gaming so that you instead reach for a puzzle, a board game, lawn games, or even old-fashioned playing cards. Our kids love UNO and SORRY ... we play these on repeat at our house. And I also love to force my family into a puzzle; everyone rolls their eyes at me, but they can't resist the temptation to join in once we get started. And if you are working a puzzle, you cannot be anywhere but present if you intend to solve the challenge.

Week 29, Day 3

<u>Get Inspired:</u>

"Beginning today, treat everyone you meet as if they were going to be dead by midnight. Extend to them all the care, kindness and understanding you can muster, and do it with no thought of any reward. Your life will never be the same again." – **Og Mandino**

<u>Get Aligned:</u>

Mindful people do not lash out at others, put them down, or step on them to raise themselves up. Mindful people can remain humble, yet steady in knowing that they have the tools to learn, grow, produce, and succeed.

Be careful not to fall into the trap of weaponizing your interactions with others. Attacking others will not improve your confidence, but it will consume your energy.

Instead, think about the tools you have at your disposal to achieve your goals. Create a list so that you have a clear inventory of your abilities and support systems. Build a positive mindset, assume a commanding presence by owning your space, take thoughtful action steps, and rally support from allies.

Above all else, adopt and use a kind mindset daily.

PART 3:

Cultivate Your Presence

"Maybe you are searching among the branches
for what only appears in the roots."

– *Maulana Rumi*

Week 29, Day 4

Get Inspired:

Presence is defined by *Webster's Dictionary* as:

"The bearing, carriage, or air of a person."

Get Aligned:

Cultivating our presence to be aligned with our desired goals in life lends support to Owning our Journey. When our energy, our thoughts, and our actions are not aligned, we are sending conflicting messages to our brain … and subliminally to those around us. People are cautious to trust us, individuals may not share as much information with us, or we might just have that "off" feeling in our belly.

Presence is not a process of being fancy, proper, or regal. Presence is the ability to believe in our thoughts, visions, and goals, and to carry ourselves in a way that also exudes that belief. We aren't afraid to be ourselves. We show up for ourselves, even in tough situations.

Cultivating Presence also means we show up for and believe in others. We extend kindness and selflessness to those in need. We set boundaries so that we aren't taken advantage of. We take care of our mind, our spirit, and our body. Presence is the aura that you carry.

Week 29, Day 5

Get Inspired:

"We convince by our presence."

-Walt Whitman

Get Aligned:

We each have a personal brand; whether you intentionally have thought about and designed it or not, you have a brand. Your brand is the culmination of thoughts and beliefs that others hold of you.

As a good leader of self, you should know your brand, and work on intentionally designing it to align with your True North / goals in life.

How we continuously show up in life, or our *presence*, is how we reinforce and sell our brand to the outside world.

Showcasing our brand to the world is essential for staying on our own path and finding success in our goals. We do not live in a bubble, and at some point, you *will need* the support, encouragement, buy-in, feedback, or reflection from others to continue your journey. These people can open doors for you, grease the wheels for you, or simply offer a shoulder to cry on when you fall and scrape your knee. They can offer nourishment or a safe place to rest when you are weary from the journey. And they can set you straight if you lose your compass.

None of this will happen, however, if we don't know our brand and show up authentically for our brand with our presence.

From the way we look to the way we talk, from the company we keep to the books we read, from the jobs we hold to the degrees we earn ... every choice we make helps to confirm our brand.

Know it.

Own it.

Live it.

Week 29, Day 6

<u>Get Inspired:</u>

"Presence is a state of inner spaciousness."

-Eckhart Tolle

<u>Get Aligned:</u>

Image in you are in a crowded house where every nook and cranny is filled with decorations, furniture, art, trinkets, etc. You hardly have room to move because stuff is all around you.

In this crowded house, you sense that the owner cannot decide what their style is, or what has value and what doesn't. They continue to add more and more in hopes of finding the right "look" or decorating theme … but it becomes cluttered, and the owner's style message is unclear.

This house lacks presence.

Now imagine a beautifully appointed home, with space to move around, a clear decorative theme, obvious pieces of furniture and art which you can appreciate because they are spaced apart.

This house exudes presence.

Consider your being as your "house".

How do you want to design your house? Crowded, unclear, and cluttered with random patterns and ideas. Or organized, thematic, consistent, and spacious.

When we develop presence, we are creating inner spaciousness to breathe, to reflect, and to invest ourselves into our goals. We know what we stand for, what we believe in, and what we are pursuing in life. We show up consistently for ourselves and our commitments.

If your house is currently too crowded, begin to pare it down. Slowly but surely develop the space to enjoy that which matters to you.

Week 29, Day 7

Reflect:

What inspired you this week?

What will you carry forward?

Week 30, Day 1

Get Inspired:

Newton's 2nd and 3rd Laws of Physics speak to change.

The 2nd Law states that the rate of change of momentum of an object is directly proportional to the force applied. *The 3rd Law* explains a particular symmetry in nature: forces always occur in pairs, and one body cannot exert a force on another without experiencing a force itself.

Get Aligned:

From these laws, we can see that change in our lives is directly impacted by our choices, and also by the choices of others. Sometimes we initiate the force of change, and sometimes it is initiated upon us. Not everything is in our control, however, we always have a choice of how we will REACT to the forces of change around us. Hang onto that choice and appreciate its power.

~

When the force of change is directed at us without inviting it, be sure to consider what good may come from an explosive or negative reaction on your part. Each time we choose calm and rational reactions over explosive ones, we are sharing that energy with others.

Week 30, Day 2

<u>Get Inspired:</u>

In ancient Greece there were lecture halls called *Scholeion* which served as a place for students to contemplate living a better life and weighing those concepts against the priorities of the outside world.

<u>Get Aligned:</u>

When is the last time you slowed down enough to consider your life priorities, and to compare those with how you are living and with what is being demanded of you by the outside world?

Consider how you want to show up in this world and make space to live in that value every day. When we show up authentically aligned with our intentions, that is the process of developing a grounded presence to support our Own Journey.

~

Encourage others to consider what their life priorities are by simply asking the question. The more we normalize this type of conversation the more people will take a pause to consider their priorities!

Week 30, Day 3

Get Inspired:

"Leaders create culture. Culture inspires behavior. Behavior drives results."

-Urban Meyer

Get Aligned:

As you seek to Own Your Journey through life, you will want to know and live in a culture that resonates with your soul. When you do this, your behavior will follow in accordance with your values. And when your behavior stays consistent, the results will begin to take shape.

When I was first leaving Corporate America to begin my own coaching and consulting business, it was exciting, and scary. It was all up to ME to produce.

I made sure I was very clear on my WHY of starting a company; what did I want the day-to-day operations to look like, what were my key values, what was the purpose of my work? That was setting the culture for my future.

Next, I focused in on logistics. What did I need to do every day to ensure that the results would follow? I listed out my KPIs and still keep a tracking journal to ensure that I stay on pace. These habits were the behaviors that aligned with the overall mission or culture of the company.

And finally, with consistent behaviors and habits in place, the results started to come. Clients trusted in me, they were meeting their goals, and therefore I was meeting mine.

This concept of culture – behavior – results is not limited to our work lives. It applies to raising children, to supporting a cause, and to our education.

How you show up each day matters. Keep it simple and follow the formula to ensure that your behavior drives results because it is designed by your culture.

Week 30, Day 4

Get Inspired:

"Being willing to disagree because you care is the greatest sign of respect you can show others."

-Kim Scott

Get Aligned:

Being a "yes-girl" or a "yes-guy" can be dangerous. We are setting ourselves up for a lifetime pattern of agreeing to things before we discern if they are wise, helpful, kind, productive, or even sustainable.

If you are brave enough to pause and listen to what others are saying or asking, you can take a moment to reflect on the actual content of the message. If it is not aligned with your beliefs, your abilities, your gut instinct, your priorities, or your purpose, it is OK to disagree and discuss. It shows how deeply you have been listening, it shows that you are willing to discuss the topic in depth. This is indeed a sign of respect, to truly listen to others and politely disagree.

~

When was the last time that you had a disagreement? Did you speak open mindedly from a place of candor and trust, or did you become aggressive? If you had an internal disagreement, but failed to verbalize it, consider why. What could have happened if you decided to speak up and share your point of view?

Owning Your Journey requires that you take a stance on things that matter to you. It does NOT require you to be rude or dismissive of others; but instead to be open-minded, willing to discuss, and share your thoughts. If you fail to do this, you are not truly on your own journey, but you are trailing along someone else's.

Week 30, Day 5

Get Inspired:

"The price of excellence is discipline. The cost of mediocrity is disappointment."

-William Arthur Ward

Get Aligned:

As a leader dedicated to Owning Your Journey, your job is to show up with a presence that supports your mission.

Personal Checkpoint:

Be honest, where are you lacking in self-discipline?

Your eating habits, procrastination, exercise, over sleeping, vices, money-management, time-management, relationships, authenticity, follow-through?

The list is long, and we all have natural weak spots.

Identify your weak points and do something about them.

It won't be fun, and likely won't feel good until you make new habits … but this investment is worthwhile.

Week 30, Day 6

<u>Get Inspired:</u>

Emotions are merely chemical messengers signaling through our bodies to let us know if they are pleased or uncomfortable with a situation. Emotions are not permanent, and they do not define you.

What defines you is how you REACT to your emotions.

<u>Get Aligned:</u>

Your emotions are always valid. They are signals to your brain, and should be noted, but nothing else. Don't get wrapped up in them because they are fleeting; they are not tangible.

When you find you are overly invested in your emotions, ask yourself why? Next, challenge yourself to consider a different point of view and move on.

You will be less anxious and reactive by allowing emotions to flow naturally through you and pass out of you, without gripping them in a death hold.

Exhibit emotional intelligence by acknowledging your emotions and having a responsible reaction to them. By recognizing that 'emotions' are simply a moment in time which has already passed you take away their perceived power.

How you show up in life defines how you live your life.

Week 30, Day 7

<u>Reflect:</u>

What inspired you this week?

What will you carry forward?

Week 31, Day 1

<u>Get Inspired:</u>

"In work, do what you enjoy. In family life, be completely present."

-Lao Tzu

<u>Get Aligned:</u>

In these simple words to live by, we are again reminded how challenging it can be to apply simple ideas to modern life. First, as always, we must take stock of how we are living.

Do you enjoy your work? Or do you often have the Sunday-Scaries as you prepare for the week? Step 1- consider what is and what is not working for you at work. Take steps to make changes or change your job. Of note, your work doesn't always need to be your life's calling. It is OK for your work to simply pay the bills and afford you the lifestyle to provide for your family, to travel the world, or to volunteer your time and efforts for those in need. It should not, however, feel as though it is sucking the life out of you. If you need to learn a skill to level up, then do so without complaint.

When it comes to your family, are you truly present when you are with them? We are not on this earth to "live to work", we are here to "work to live". Remember this and cling to it daily! There is no prize at your death bed for being the hardest worker or the most dedicated to answering emails as quickly as they arrive.

Set the example that family does take precedence over work at the end of the day (and sometimes during the day), and that work will take precedence over family "after hours" *only* when there is a true emergency.

Take a day off to chaperone your child's field trip. Silence your calls/emails so that you can enjoy a dinner with your love or with a friend. Use your weekend to truly recharge and disconnect. Organize a "community day" for your team, where work is on hold, and you are focused on doing good for others.

Be clear and consistent in how you show up. Your thoughtful presence will further bolster your efforts to Own Your Journey.

Week 31, Day 2

<u>Get Inspired:</u>

Leadership guru, John Maxwell, talks about the different *styles of leadership* that we can use to trigger peak performance in others. These four key styles include:

<u>Leadership style #1</u>: encourage significance.

<u>Leadership style #2</u>: share in the big picture.

<u>Leadership style #3</u>: bench stacking.

<u>Leadership style #4</u>: clear communication & good listening.

~

- *4 Leadership Styles That Trigger Peak Performance,* by John Maxwell, JohnMaxwell.com, September 29, 2015

<u>Get Aligned:</u>

Following these guidelines, we can extrapolate that if we embrace these same four styles within our Own Journey of self-leadership, we will inspire ourselves to peak performance.

#1: Define your big dream, and then design a team of individuals who would be beneficial to and want to join your efforts towards that dream. Encourage them to join you, and you will lend significance and urgency to the dream.

#2: Serve something bigger than yourself. Reward and recognize others, support others, encourage others. Your selfless behaviors are an asset to self-leadership because they keep us humble and aware of the big picture.

#3: Always be looking to develop the people who aren't necessarily on the frontlines. By believing in and supporting these people, you will again be selfless, and others will naturally want to support you in return. These will be the individuals who step up to help you along your Own Journey when needed.

#4: Being a good listener is key to being a good leader. Therefore, as a leader of self we must also listen to our own hearts and minds. Trust your gut instincts, listen to your concerns, give space for your big dreams to find their voice. This is the only true way forward to Own your Journey.

~

Your presence as a leader of self will greatly impact your progress of Owning Your Journey.

Week 31, Day 3

Get Inspired:

"Beware the barrenness of a busy life."

-Socrates

Get Aligned:

Busy is a buzz word that has a cult-like following. We wear it as a martyr's badge, proud of our exhaustion.

But in reality, "busy" means that you are refusing to take control of your schedule, and instead are letting the world run you ragged without prioritizing how you spend your time.

Do you use the phrase "Oh I'm so busy"? Try to shift that statement. Experiment with "I've had a wonderfully full plate" or "I've been fortunate to have a steady pipeline of work" or "The kids are grabbing life by the horns, and I am excited to be there supporting them". The shift in tone takes back your power over your choice of how to spend your time. It shows gratitude for the many experiences you are embracing.

If you are in a down / difficult period of life, it can and should be acknowledged. It is OK to say "I've honestly been struggling to keep my head above water, I can't seem to catch my breath.". This more honest and clear perspective will open the window of discussion surrounding HOW you can make a change.

Week 31, Day 4

Get Inspired:

"There are only two days in the year that nothing can be done. One is called yesterday and the other is called tomorrow, so today is the right day to love, believe, do and mostly live."

– Dalai Lama

Get Aligned:

If you are like many of us, you spend a good portion of your day thinking about what you will do or need to do tomorrow, this week, and further into the future. You may also spend time replaying events from the past, wondering why you made a specific choice or wishing you could have a re-do. All of this takes precious energy away from the NOW.

It is worth considering if all the planning and reflecting is a means to avoid the present. Most of the angst we carry is self-made when we stay stuck in our minds on the hamster wheel of "what if..." or "if only I had..."

What would happen if you lived fully in the present?

Likely, you would be more engaged in each interaction you have. You would find more joy in the moments that fill your day. Your glimpses of boredom may allow you to see details around you that were previously missed.

Week 31, Day 5

Get Inspired:

Radical Candor is the idea that the intersection of Caring Personally + Challenging Directly is the most effective way to exhibit candor.

-As taught by **Kim Scott**

Get Aligned:

Pursuing *Radical Candor* at work, as the boss, or at home as a parent is commendable. It is a skill set that doesn't come easy but will empower your relationships over the long term.

Have you ever paused to consider the amount of radical candor that you extend to yourself along your personal journey of life?

In her book, *Radical Candor*, Scott shares the steps to show up with radical candor in all our relationships.

Step 1 indicates that we must *Care Personally*. That requires us to put care, concern, and attention towards our needs, dreams, and goals.

Step 2 is *Challenging Directly*. That step requires us to look in the mirror with deep self-awareness to ensure we aren't being lazy, self-centered, fearful, hateful, or a slew of other negative realities.

She goes on to point out the matrix of Caring and Challenging, and how the combination will impact our attempts to engage with others.

When we exhibit <u>caring without challenging</u>, we land in the space of *ruinous empathy* (a refusal to call a spade a spade for fear of hurting feelings).

When we exhibit <u>low personal care with low challenging</u>, we fall into a pattern of *manipulative insecurity* (you become overly obsessed with protecting your feelings).

When we exhibit <u>low care with high challenge</u>, we can exert *obnoxious aggression* (loudly pointing out a failure).

Only when we have <u>high care and high challenge</u> do we show up with *radical candor*, acknowledging a situation that is "off" and doing so in a supportive manner.

~

For our personal journey, it is necessary that we call ourselves to the carpet in difficult situations, but also talk ourselves through how to rectify the mistake or improve going forward. We must always seek to exhibit radical candor when we are attempting to improve our self-leadership.

Week 31, Day 6

Get Inspired:

"For those who have experienced the joy of being alone with nature there is really little need for me to say much more; for those who have not, no words of mine can ever describe the powerful, almost mystical knowledge of beauty and eternity that come, suddenly, and all unexpected."

-Jane Goodall

Get Aligned:

If you have never taken the time to be still in Nature, you are missing one of the most awe-inspiring events in life. Nature is a great teacher and listener. Nature helps our minds, and our hearts heal. Nature provides space to spark your creativity and to think through your roadblocks. We should all make space to be alone in Nature every day in some small capacity.

Not sure where to begin? Sunrise and sunset are magical times and happen every day! They are a great place to start by simply spending five to fifteen minutes staying still and watching the show unfold before you. There is a powerful calming and simultaneously inspiring feeling that comes from witnessing either phenomenon.

Week 31, Day 7

<u>Reflect:</u>

What inspired you this week?

What will you carry forward?

Week 32, Day 1

Get Inspired:

"Presence is more than just being there."

-Malcolm S. Forbes

Get Aligned:

Anyone can BE there. Just physically being in a space does not mean that you have cultivated presence. We must go beyond the physical, to be mentally engaged, emotionally be engaged, remain inquisitive, be a cheerleader, be a problem solver, and be a question asker.

Presence is: showing up in all aspects to align our physical appearance, our mindset, our actions, our thoughts, and our engagement with a specific situation.

As we pursue our Own Journey in life, we will be called and pulled in millions of directions. If you are constantly jumping towards each ringing bell, you will struggle to cultivate a presence for anything. Occasionally we need to slow down long enough to ask ourselves, *why are we jumping at everything*? We should reconsider the vision that we have constructed for how we want to live our lives, for what is important and essential to us, and then to ensure that we are cultivating a presence to support those key aspects of life.

If we are a doer of all things, we will struggle to be masters of our own lives.

Week 32, Day 2

Get Inspired:

"If your presence doesn't make an impact, your absence won't make a difference."

-Trey Smith

Get Aligned:

Have you ever found yourself in a training session at work, but you are making notes for a future meeting, cleaning up email, or otherwise disengaged? What about those times when you are playing Legos with your child and find yourself flipping through text messages or social media with your second hand.

In these moments, we are not truly there if only our body is present.

This is a strong reminder that our presence is a full body commitment to something. If we are bothering to give a situation our time, why then are we not going all in with our brain and our attention? Time is not a renewable resource; we only get so much. To be exact, we get only 1,440 minutes each day... and hopefully 30% of those minutes are spent sleeping.

When we commit our time, we should be double checking with ourselves to ensure that we create a presence that WOULD be missed if we aren't there. This is how you show up as a leader in life.

Week 32, Day 3

Get Inspired:

"I don't lose my temper; I use my temper."

-Dolly Parton

Get Aligned:

When asked about being such a nice person, Dolly responded to interviewers explaining that she keeps her cool unless you mess with her family or her business, at which point she intentionally creates a presence to use her temper as a vehicle to convey her intensity.

Be aware of how you show up. Are you known as the "emotional" person who reacts to situations with great intensity? Are you the "stoic" person who never reacts and is always sporting a poker face? Or do you land somewhere in the middle?

I think we are all hoping to fall somewhere in the middle. To be open minded and approachable while maintaining our emotional intelligence when frustrated or challenged. And reserving our temper (as Dolly puts it) for moments when we really want to make an impact. If we are overly reactive on a regular basis, people will begin to ignore us because they have grown numb or annoyed with our explosive presence. If we are never reactive, people will have a hard time trusting us because we refuse to display any personal emotions. Take the time to pay attention to how you show up, and make adjustments if necessary, so that you are aligned in your presence with how you intend to show up.

Week 32, Day 4

Get Inspired:

"Sometimes we're so concerned about not hurting someone's feelings, that we wind up at what I call 'ruinous empathy'."

-**Kim Scott**, *The Talent Grow Show*, episode 177

Get Aligned:

Being kind is a wonderful attribute that should never be set aside. We should always strive to be kind in our connections and our feedback to others. However, when we are overly empathetic to others without being brave enough to be honest, we are going along with a false narrative in our own minds. This is very disruptive to our sense of right and wrong, and to our internal compass which is trying to remain fixed at True North.

This is also unfair to the person with whom we are exhibiting "ruinous empathy"; we are letting them believe that we agree and support their actions or thoughts, when in fact we do not.

A prime example of this is the new-aged concept of "participation trophies" for our children. We are so afraid for them to lose that as a society we have decided that every child should receive an award for merely showing up. We are not teaching them to fail forward. We are not teaching them the truth in life that, even though you work hard, you still might not be the best or even recognized for your efforts. When are we preserving these lessons for? I see no problem with awarding "best team spirit" or "most improved" or cleanest uniform" awards for kids at the end of a sports season; but absolutely see the general category of "participation trophies" as a gateway to feeding our adult sense of "ruinous empathy".

Be true to your instincts, your thoughts, and your ideas. When it is time to disagree with someone or to let them know that they are not the winner, be kind and respectful, but be honest.

Week 32, Day 5

Get Inspired:

"Leadership is about making others better as a result of your presence and making sure that impact lasts in your absence."

-Sheryl Sandberg

Get Aligned:

As a parent, raising children is the first place that this quote takes me. Our role as parents is to be a good leader to our children, to set an example of how to lead oneself, and to help them become good members of society.

It also applies directly to any formal work situation, to informal mentorships, and to your efforts in the community.

To be a good leader to others, we must show up authentically and with engagement. This is also incredibly true for our desire to be a leader of self. We must be authentic and honest with ourselves, we must be attentive and actively engaged in what we are committed to, and we must embrace the micro-habits that will allow us to continue this journey with sustainable amounts of effort.

When we show up for ourselves, we should be supporting the key areas of our being:

Physical Health, Emotional Health, Family Engagement, Hobbies & Life Experiences, Grounded Home, Spiritual Contentment, Relationships with Friends, and Professional Path.

If any of these areas are lacking your supportive presence, you have the power to change that. You can focus on and fully show up in a way that feels good to you for each of these areas of your life.

Week 32, Day 6

Get Inspired:

"It is not about win or lose, it is about do you accept the challenge."
— Matthew McConaughey

Get Aligned:

If you aren't willing to cowboy up in life, you are eventually going to miss the ride of a lifetime. The trick is, you never know which ride will be "the one", so you've got to risk falling a few times to get to the good stuff.

Be a person of conviction. Try in the face of fear. Breathe, show up, and do your best. It will demonstrate to you what you are really made of.

Week 32, Day 7

Reflect:

What inspired you this week?

What will you carry forward?

Week 33, Day 1

Get Inspired:

"Nothing ever goes away until it has taught us what we need to know."

-Pema Chödrön

Get Aligned:

And so it is, that hard lessons follow us around until we seem to absorb them.

If you continue to face a similar situation repeatedly, perhaps it is time for you to look in the mirror and discover what is really going on?

Do you have friendships that fizzle out? Perhaps you are hanging out with the wrong people, or perhaps you are not as good of a friend to others as you think.

Do you keep missing that next promotion? Perhaps you are trying to move forward with the wrong company, or perhaps you are not putting in the work to improve specific skills that are required for that next-level job.

Are you constantly fighting with your kids? Perhaps you are not communicating with clarity, or perhaps you are not investing the time in them that you should.

Do you find yourself frantic to meet deadlines (large or small)? Perhaps you need to consider if you are disorganized, or perhaps you have taken on too many responsibilities.

There is a lesson in each challenge we face. The question is, will we listen and learn the first time?

Week 33, Day 2

Get Inspired:

Embrace the 'Daily Power 5': MIRAA

1. Movement
2. Intention
3. Rest
4. Affirm
5. Appreciate

Get Aligned:

The Daily Power 5 is a notion that I reflected on over the years of coaching many high achieving individuals. I have often seen that the most successful and happy people are thriving in all 5 areas. These are markers of how we show up, and how we move forward in life. Take a moment to do a personal analysis of yourself.

~

1. **Movement**: Exercise your body to stimulate your brain. Move each day. A body in motion stays in motion, as a body at rest dies more quickly.
2. **Intention**: Visualize your intentions; Plan and organize your priorities.
3. **Rest**: Grant your body time to heal with sleep and disconnected space.
4. **Affirm**: Believe in yourself and say it out loud.
5. **Appreciate**: Gratitude statements will keep you grounded, humble, and positive in your outlook.

How you show up for your life each day is a reflection of how you are leading yourself.

Week 33, Day 3

Get Inspired:

"In your calm is your strength."

-German Proverb

Get Aligned:

One of our greatest challenges in life is to learn how to react to the rush of emotions that we feel during intense times. We can be a slave to them, or we can work to logically navigate them.

Being passionate about something will make it likely that you will have a large emotional reaction to that situation. However, a true leader of self will know the difference between Feeling the emotion and Reacting to the emotion.

When you are able to separate the two, you are then able to tap into a place of calm. This calm is indeed your strength; it provides you with the ability to take a pause before you react, to look objectively at a situation, and to avoid being a victim of your emotions.

Week 33, Day 4

<u>Get Inspired:</u>

"Within groups of people, there are alpha and beta personalities. Alphas are the leaders, and ally with strong betas. Betas don't seek a role as the leader, but do want the influence or power that comes by association to the leader. You will also find the vast majority of people who are neither alpha or beta; these people have no desire to exert influence and are comfortable with staying securely in the pack.

Of note, male alphas tend to promote their own achievements and rise to places of formal leadership. Female alphas are more focused with influence on a group, and less on the title or position she holds."

-Owen Eastwood, *Belonging: The Ancient Code of Togetherness,* Quercus Publishing, 2021, pg. 195-6.

<u>Get Aligned:</u>

Recognizing and acknowledging how you prefer to show up in a group is key to developing strong self-leadership. Being honest with yourself about how you prefer to navigate the politics of a group or team will help you to find a comfortable space, and to interact more effectively and authentically with others.

Reflect on your current social groups, and consider your role now, as well as the role that would be most comfortable for you. Use this self-awareness as you consider opportunities for engagement within any setting.

Learn to recognize how other alphas and betas show up. Be prepared to harmoniously interact with them in a way that makes you <u>both</u> feel comfortable.

If you are an alpha, you can easily coexist with other alphas. There is often more than one in any given group. Having awareness is key to understanding the unspoken politics so that you don't become frustrated with communications throughout the group.

Week 33, Day 5

<u>Get Inspired:</u>

"The secret to beauty is simple – be who you are."

— Bobbi Brown

<u>Get Aligned:</u>

Knowing your unique brand is essential to living a life that feels authentic and one that also helps you to achieve your goals. It is hard to "sell" yourself if you aren't in touch with what your brand is.

If you truly know who you are, what you believe, what makes you happy and sad, what excites you, what scares you, what you enjoy … then your personal beauty will shine through. We are so steeped in stimuli that we fail to remember our incredible capacity as humans to listen to our instincts. Have you ever met someone who just left you feeling as though you couldn't read them? We generally don't like to be around people like that; as humans, we want to know our tribe and know where we stand within the tribe. It is one of our evolutionary traits designed to keep us safe.

Simply being clear about who you are will attract others to you because they can *trust* your authentic presence.

Not sure where you stand on this topic? Answer these fun questions in rapid fire, and then keep the list going with more of your own.

PS- This is for fun, don't take yourself so seriously!

1. Jewel tones or pastels
2. Nature or modern comforts
3. Loud or soft music
4. Big crowds or intimate conversations
5. Start-ups or corporate giants
6. Left-wing or right-wing
7. Omnivore or vegetarian
8. Couch potato or exercise
9. Travel adventures or lasting traditions
10. Movies or musicals
11. Pets or no pets
12. Sunset or sunrise
13. Preppy or boho
14. Listener or talker
15. Analytical or quick decisions

Get clear on who you are and allow your presence to be authentic.

Week 33, Day 6

Get Inspired:

"You are unique and your purpose is to live your uniqueness."

-Milena Karanovic

Get Aligned:

If you spend your efforts trying to fit in, to be one of the sheep in the herd, you will forever be pulling energy away from your unique qualities. We all look differently, think differently, and act differently. This is what makes life interesting. Why then, would you put effort into taking that away?

Once you become comfortable with who you really are, you can show up with an authentic presence. This is when you will finally make progress on achieving the goals and ideals that are truly aligned with your vision of success in life.

Another bonus of having an authentic presence? People will trust you.

We still retain our pre-historic abilities to gauge the authenticity of other humans. When we sense that something is not in alignment (for example: maybe your body language and your words don't tell the same story), we pull back and are less trusting of this "less than clear" individual. Living in authenticity means that your energy, your message, and your presence are all aligned ... and you will begin to build trust with others.

Week 33, Day 7

<u>Reflect:</u>

What inspired you this week?

What will you carry forward?

Week 34, Day 1

Get Inspired:

"You, yourself, as much as anybody in the entire universe, deserve your love and affection."

-Buddha

Get Aligned:

As the stewards on the airplane say, "We must first place the oxygen mask on ourselves before attempting to help others".

If you are unwilling to invest positively in yourself, there will be less of you to share with others.

If you fail to respect yourself, why would you expect anyone else to?

Notice the tiny ways that you ignore or put yourself down each day. Are you caring for your physical health, mental health, and emotional health? Are you infusing joy into your life, and believing in yourself?

If not, start making changes today.

Banish the excuse that "you don't have time". Everyone has time for one more glass of water each day, or to squeeze in 10minutes of stretching, or to choose a healthy snack over processed garbage. Battle back when your brain tells you that you aren't good enough; list an example or two of things you have accomplished. Write a love note to yourself, detailing a few amazing things that make you special.

~

Spreading the Love:

Ask your kids what they love about themselves. Train them early to value their strengths while also remaining humble.

Encourage your team in self-care by offering a weekly team walk or mediation practice over lunch.

Write a letter to yourself 10 years in the future. Be sure to save it and open it on that date!

Week 34, Day 2

Get Inspired:

Hang out with people who are kicking ass and who will make you feel like a giant loser if you're not kicking ass too!

— Jen Sincero

Get Aligned:

If you are serious about leveling up your game and your self-leadership qualities, surround yourself with people whom you want to be like. I'm not saying you should try to be someone else, but you will want to absorb their energy to help promote your own energy to a higher level of vibration.

Your tribe will have an impact on your vibe.

If you want to level up, limit your time with people who are pessimistic about life, who want to do as little as possible, or who generally look down on others.

Seek out those who have a positive outlook, who believe in abundance, who share their gifts, who challenge themselves, and who don't make excuses.

~

The energy of the tribe you choose strongly impacts your vibe and presence in this world.

Week 34, Day 3

Get Inspired:

"Relying on each other is a sound survival strategy for a frail, noisy creature without a lot of built-in weapons. Living in groups is a ticket to survival, which is why most primates live in them."

-David Berreby, "Why Do We See So Many Things As 'Us vs. Them'?", *National Geographic*, 12 March 2018.

Get Aligned:

As humans, our superpower is the ability to form strongly bonded and effective living groups. In centuries past, rejection from a group mean imminent death for an individual. And so, we have a deep need to fit in and find our tribe built into our DNA.

Be cautious not to join a 'tribe' simply because they welcome you. Instead, lean into next-level-self-leadership by considering if this tribe has similar morals, goals, and work ethics as you. If not, keep looking.

As a leader, consider your own psychological impact on others. Don't be the one to isolate another human unnecessarily. Remember what your mother used to say, "if you have nothing nice to say, simply say nothing at all".

Week 34, Day 4

Get Inspired:

"I've learned that people will forget what you said, people will forget what you did, but people will never forget how you made them feel."

— Maya Angelou

Get Aligned:

Every encounter with another human or living creature is an opportunity to show up with kindness, or with disregard.

When we are having a bad day, it can be difficult to extend kindness or grace to those around us. But acting with kindness actually *fills* our bucket, rather than depleting it. When you choose to treat others in a positive manner, you unleash a river of positive energy which will serve that individual, and yourself.

Making others feel welcomed, safe, loved, heard, empowered, strong, capable, or appreciated does not take an extreme effort or gesture on your part. A smile, a wave, a note, a kind word, or a moment of your time is all that it takes.

How we treat others reflects who we truly are.

Week 34, Day 5

<u>Get Inspired:</u>

"Positive emotional energy is the key to health, happiness and wellbeing. The more positive you are, the better your life will be in every area."

-Brian Tracy

<u>Get Aligned:</u>

Your energy impacts your presence, which in turn impacts your ability to Own Your Journey. Growing as you go is important to developing the presence you desire; your growth process is cyclical and has larger impacts down the road than it likely does now.

For example, if you want to cultivate a better ability to communicate and connect with others, begin by building personal awareness of how you show up. Practice paying attention to how others show up. Be flexible in your communication style so that you encounter fewer challenges and hiccups in your effort to connect with others.

As you grow in this "invisible skill", you will attract a wide variety of people, likely including the ones whom you are trying to connect with. From there, your success as a leader grows exponentially as you are able to touch people's lives in a meaningful, productive, and connected manner.

Applying this concept to your practice of self-leadership, your growth still determines who you attract. Who you attract will determine the success of your ability to meet goals that you set forth for yourself.

Your presence resonates with an energy which others are attracted (or repelled from). We must build our tribe with the right people, as those around us can have a powerful impact on our ability to follow our true North.

Week 34, Day 6

Get Inspired:

"Don't use your energy to worry. Use your energy to believe."

Joel Osteen

Get Aligned:

As has been referenced many times, your energy not only impacts your mindset, it also bleeds through and shows itself in your presence. When we waste time steeped in worry, we carry an uneasy energy. This invisible force makes us less desirable to be around and limits our ability to move forward in the world.

When we use our energy to believe in our vision, our goals, and our passions in life, we are maximizing our energy frequency and attracting more abundance.

Recall that the Law of Attraction states that like attracts like. If you want to be in the company of productive, kind, and positive people … you must show up in a similar energy. When you show up using your resource of energy in a negative manner, you will only attract more negative events in your life.

Week 34, Day 7

Reflect:

What inspired you this week?

What will you carry forward?

Week 35, Day 1

<u>Get Inspired:</u>

Years back I developed a formula for what I lovingly refer to as the *Steppingstones of Success*. These are the skill sets in life that can lift us up to our next-level or can serve as tripping hazards that hold us back. They are as follows:

Voice

Confidence

Fear

Focus

Resilience

Harmony

<u>Get Aligned:</u>

In the coming pages, we will explore concepts around each of these Steppingstones. The skills learned will help to bolster a positive presence so that you can show up to life authentically and with clarity.

Voice:

The ability to use your voice to share your ideas, connect with others effectively, and remain engaged.

Confidence:

Learning to let go of perfectionism, banishing Imposter Syndrome, and beginning to trust in yourself.

Fear:

The ability to move forward in the face of fear, and to adapt the ability to Fail Forward (applying lessons from our challenges to leverage ourselves forward next time).

Focus:

Quieting the noise and distractions so that you achieve your goals, and to reduce procrastination.

Resilience:

Balancing the combination of Grit (sticking to it), Grace (acknowledging that you aren't perfect, nor do you have to be), and Space (time and space to recover and rest).

Harmony:

Ditching the belief that life is Balanced, and instead embracing the idea of Harmony that will flow in different ways through different seasons of life, while finding joy with your life.

Week 35, Day 2

Get Inspired:

"If you don't use your voice, there's someone waiting behind you who will."

-Kat Cole

Get Aligned:

Your voice is a powerful instrument. It is often one that we must get comfortable using, and therefore it takes practice.

Don't muffle your voice; instead, be proud of what you must share with the world and be heard.

Practice by first thinking through what you want to say, and then sharing your thoughts in a concise and clear manner.

To be impactful, don't wrap your words in veils of secrecy. Come out and say what you mean. Upon sharing, always be open to the flow of exchange back and forth. It's not about having the last word, but it is about sharing ideas.

Your voice is a vehicle for your energy. Use it as you navigate along Your Own Journey.

Week 35, Day 3

<u>Get Inspired:</u>

"The only way to find your voice is to use it."

-Austin Kleon

<u>Get Aligned:</u>

Some people are born with the gift of gab. They seem infinitely comfortable talking in any company, about almost any topic. I know because *I* am that chatty person.

Others seem unsure of how or when to use their voice. And another group of people exists; those who see no purpose in adding their voice to an already busy conversation.

But every voice matters. And every voice is unique.

Get started by simply harnessing the power of questions.

Not sure what to say? Ask a clarifying or detail seeking question as a follow-up to the person talking. This opens the doors for more exchange of information.

If you are the chatty one, work to intentionally invite others into the conversation.

If you are the quiet one, work to intentionally interject thoughts or questions into the conversation.

Week 35, Day 4

<u>Get Inspired:</u>

"Connection is why we're here; it is what gives purpose and meaning to our lives. The power that connection holds in our lives was confirmed when the main concern about connection emerged as the fear of disconnection; the fear that something we have done or failed to do, something about who we are or where we come from, has made us unlovable and unworthy of connection."

- **Brené Brown**, *Daring Greatly*

<u>Get Aligned:</u>

Perhaps one of our greatest tools in life is the ability to connect deeply with others. COIVD showed us quickly how important the sense of connection was to our collective wellbeing.

So how does one begin to develop deeper connections?

1- Authenticity & Vulnerability
2- Listening well
3- Flexibility

When we show up authentically without fear of being vulnerable, we invite others to see the real us. This creates an unconscious level of trust. Have you ever met that person whom you struggle to know "their agenda" because they come across as guarded? It begins to make you question everything you say and do in front of them, and to put up barriers. Authenticity and vulnerability are the opposite of this. Be genuine and put down your armor.

When we are truly listening, this is an active process. We aren't thinking 2 steps ahead about what WE want to say; we are engaged and engrossed in what the other person has to share. And we listen with more than our ears. Our eyes are constantly searching for clues to let us know what the other person is saying. If you are engaging with another human (or animal), take the time to make eye contact, to focus your body on them, and to actively hear what is being said.

Perhaps the most advanced skill in learning to communicate is the ability to be flexible. To be aware of how the other person is showing up, and to flex in your communication style to align more closely with them. I'm not saying you should change who you are but taking the time to bridge the gap between two different communication styles is supremely powerful when working to develop efficient communication.

Week 35, Day 5

Get Inspired:

"The true purpose of a present is to be received."

-Marie Kondo

Get Aligned:

When you are offered a compliment or credit for your work, how do you react?

Do you downplay the compliment? Do you refuse kind words? Do you ignore it out of embarrassment?

Each of these reactions is actually a rude rebuff to the giver.

Train yourself to simply say "thank you".

By refusing a compliment extended towards us, we are essentially throwing a gift back in the giver's face. Mind your manners and learn to humbly accept a compliment, even if you feel it is undeserved. You are welcome to acknowledge the efforts of others, but don't fail to first extend a 'thank you' to the giver.

Having the presence to remain humble while simultaneously allowing others to acknowledge your efforts is a skill that many great leaders of self continuously struggle with. Pay attention, remain self-aware, and keep it simple.

Week 35, Day 6

Get Inspired:

"Worry gives small things a big shadow."

-Swedish Proverb

Get Aligned:

It is a proverbial dance. We get stressed or worried about something, and then we latch onto it with force; this act alone increases our biological stress responses.

When you find a challenging situation, pause to ask yourself "Do I really have any control over this situation? And if not, why am I wasting time stressing over it?". As humans, we love control. We want to know the outcomes before we begin.

We must learn to relinquish some fear of the unknown and trust that we are doing our best for any given situation.

Week 35, Day 7

<u>Reflect:</u>

What inspired you this week?

What will you carry forward?

Week 36, Day 1

Get Inspired:

"Communication – the human connection – is the key to personal and career success."

-Paul J. Meyer

Get Aligned:

From getting your toddler to eat their veggies, to inspiring the soccer team, to living in bliss with your spouse, to leading a team at work … communication is the lynch pin that often determines success in each of these scenarios. So many of us have wonderful ideas but fail to communicate the vision and/or the process and outcomes. When we don't supply the full story, we are missing the "hook" that invites people to actively listen and consider what we are saying.

Humans are still, at their core, visual thinkers. Our brains love a story line which they can turn into a mini movie reel. Once we learn how to communicate with people in a way that makes us seen and heard, we can inspire incredible change and action in the world around us!

The key is learning to connect with people on a deeper level. We must pay attention to how others naturally prefer to communicate, and flex to meet their needs. Think of it like this: Your message is a gift … but for people to be curious enough to unwrap the gift, it needs to be presented in a manner that speaks to *them*. Some prefer plain kraft paper with a starchy white bow. Some love a sparkly bag with tulle and confetti. Others are drawn to geometric prints with a neon bow.

The point is - you aren't wrapping the gift (your message) for yourself. Wrap it in a way that attracts and interests the desired person/audience for your message. Be flexible in how you approach others so that they *want* to hear your message.

We must also be sure to share the key details, and not keep others in the dark. We share by inviting others to actively participate in the conversation, by giving and taking turns.

When we do this, we can ignite a storm of possibility that others want to explore.

Week 36, Day 2

Get Inspired:

"There's power in allowing yourself to be known and heard, in owning your unique story, in using your authentic voice."

– Michelle Obama

Get Aligned:

Despite their husband's varied popularities, the American people have a long history of generally embracing and respecting our First Ladies (minus a few standouts). One of the most popular of those was Michelle Obama, who has consistently ranked in the Top 10 of various popularity polls. As First Lady, Obama used her platform to focus on poverty awareness, education, physical activity, and balanced nutrition.

As a woman married to the President of the United States, she found a way to have her own platform, to share her unique voice, and to create her own group of loyal followers. This comes from her willingness to be unique, to stand on her own ideas, and to share her voice with the world.

We may not all get a worldly platform to share our voice, but we can be brave enough to share our authentic selves within our own circles. Find your confidence by showing up with an authentic voice. Empower others by sharing who you are, and doing so in a kind way that does not put others down.

Your success does not require the failure of others. It is quite the opposite.

Your success comes from being uniquely you, allowing others to also be themselves, and moving forward confidently that others cannot impact you or tear you down unless you allow them to.

Week 36, Day 3

Get Inspired:

Science & Hormones:

Serotonin and Oxytocin are two key hormones that both work on the pre-frontal cortex (the center of higher order thinking and executive function).

Serotonin helps to regulate your mood and is connected to your personal pride.

Oxytocin is connected to comfort and deep emotional connection.

The amygdala can be referred to as the fear center of the brain.

Serotonin and Oxytocin, in elevated levels, both serve as a pacifier to quiet down the fear reaction that transpires in the amygdala.

Get Aligned:

It's not all just "in your head"; it turns out that a lot of your ability to be confident is in your hormones – the chemical messengers within our bodies.

Serotonin increases in sunlight, when we exercise, and when we have positive social interactions. Oxytocin is often referred to as the love-hormone; it increases for mothers of newborn babies to help promote bonding, when we hold hands, or even when we snuggle with someone we like.

Isolating yourself and avoiding the outdoors (aka, sunlight) will have a negative impact on your chemical ability to develop confidence.

Get out there! Be social, enjoy the outdoors, move your body. All these efforts will help to quiet the fear center so that your confidence can begin to build.

Week 36, Day 4

Get Inspired:

"Being brave isn't the absence of fear. Being brave is having that fear but finding a way through it."

-Bear Grylls

Get Aligned:

Action is the number one anecdote to a lack of confidence. When we are brave enough to act, we automatically level up our confidence.

These do not have to be grand gestures, have a simple conversation with someone that makes you nervous, take ownership of a mistake you made, or open a new bank account ear marked for your dream vacation fund.

When we take action, we take away the power of the unknown. And the unknown is truly the force that leaves us feeling insecure and nervous. You may not love the outcome, but you will know where you stand, and that gives you the freedom to move forward in life. That gives your brain the proof that you can do hard things and live to tell about it.

Week 36, Day 5

Get Inspired:

"The best way to gain self-confidence is to do what you are afraid of."

-Anonymous

Get Aligned:

In other words, the number one anecdote to Imposter Syndrome is action. Making a choice and making a move.

You are allowed to be scared and nervous.

You are allowed to have a shaky voice and trembling hands.

Do it anyway.

And when you do, the tiny building blocks of confidence will begin to amass; and next time it will be a little bit easier.

Do you want to truly Own Your Journey? If so, you must build the muscle of confidence to help carry you through the difficult times.

Week 36, Day 6

Get Inspired:

"Wisdom, Happiness, and Courage are not waiting somewhere out beyond sight at the end of a straight line; they're part of a continuous cycle that begins right here. They're not only the ending, but the beginning as well."

-Benjamin Hoff, *The Tao of Pooh*

Get Aligned:

Your presence is exactly what you believe it to be. If you think that only the future version of you is smart, funny, capable, happy, brave, ready or otherwise delightful, you will *never* get to be that person.

We must believe in ourselves TODAY. We must believe that we are smart, happy, and capable right now ... even if we have days that feel as though we are faltering on all fronts. Believing in yourself is what creates that presence for yourself. And creating that presence for yourself in turn helps you to believe in yourself.

Thought and action are cyclical in nature. Somewhere along the spectrum lies your presence. Once you begin showing up as if you believe in yourself, you will be amazed at what transpires. You will feel more confident and act with more conviction.

I am not suggesting that we show up with an arrogant stature. That is never a helpful or fruitful presence. However, believing in your ability to achieve by showing up and being consistent will free you from the doubts that hold you back in the shadows of life.

It's time to open the curtain to the sunlight and let it bathe your face!

Week 36, Day 7

<u>Reflect:</u>

What inspired you this week?

What will you carry forward?

Week 37, Day 1

Get Inspired:

Caroline Miller, an author, and psychologist, shares that a willingness to be different is crucial to building confidence.

Get Aligned:

If you are stuck on the fear-wagon of wanting to blend into the background, you will constantly struggle to find your confidence.

By acknowledging and embracing our true selves, our unique strengths, and our personal quests, we are taking a step forward for action. Recall that action is crucial for confidence to build.

When we ignore what makes us different, when we blend in with all the other ideas, there is rarely a moment of action required. We are robbing ourselves of confidence building moments.

Be present as your unique self, and in the process, you will be building self-confidence.

Week 37, Day 2

Get Inspired:

Power Pose often. If you aren't familiar with Power Posing, it is the term coined for standing (or sitting) tall in your space, channeling self-confidence, and tapping into your biology to feel that confidence. Check out **Amy Cuddy**'s 2012 Ted Talk *"Your Body Language May Shape Who You Are"*.

Get Aligned:

Girls especially are often in need of Power Posing. By the time they hit puberty, it is well documented that girls begin to shrink in their physical space. To pull back, lean in, and avoid taking up space. At the same time, the boys are naturally taking up more space, expanding, and owning their space with more vigor.

Don't believe me? Simply walk through the halls of any middle school … it is blatantly obvious in how these children move through their days.

The impacts of this biological tendency are tremendous. By the time women reach their working careers, they are often being left behind because of the mere inability to show up as confidently as their male peers.

Challenge yourself to reclaim your space. It doesn't matter if you are a man or a woman, invest in owning your bubble. Be a mentor to a younger person. If you see a teen or young adult who is shrinking back, share the Power Pose magic so that they, too, can grow.

Week 37, Day 3

Get Inspired:

"Great leaders encourage leadership development by openly developing themselves."

-Marshall Goldsmith

Get Aligned:

Looking inward and developing yourself is not a selfish act. As you look inward to be the most authentic and best version of yourself that you can be, you are modeling for those around you how to do the same for themselves.

Self-leadership doesn't happen by mistake. It is an intentional practice that lasts a lifetime. It takes focused practice and requires you to stretch out of your comfort zone as you take action to grow in a positive space.

Week 37, Day 4

<u>Get Inspired:</u>

"A confident person- knowing and believing in her identity- carries tools, not weapons."

-Amy Cuddy

<u>Get Aligned:</u>

This has long been one of my favorite quotes. It reminds us that we can be both confident and humble; that we can believe in ourselves while using tools to achieve our goals; that we do not need to step on others to get where we are going.

In short: go through life being positive and helpful as opposed to being mean and believing everyone is the potential enemy.

Are you competitive? Me too!

But being competitive doesn't mean you are working against an enemy. You can cheer others on while working your tail off to be your best, and to strategically work towards your goals without putting others down along the way.

~

Make an effort to congratulate others on their success, even if you feel of pit of longing for that same success. Over time, this will condition your brain that it is OK to celebrate others. This will begin to curb that nasty feeling of jealousy, you know, the feeling that turns you into a not-so-nice human.

At the same time, take stock of your tool kit. Do you need to add new tools or sharpen old ones in order to be confidently prepared to tackle your goals? By acknowledging this and doing the work to improve, you are showing others that it is never too late to grow and develop.

Week 37, Day 5

Get Inspired:

"And the day came when the risk to remain tight in a bud was more painful than the risk it took to blossom."

-Anaïs Nin

Get Aligned:

By nature, we are designed to protect ourselves. Even if we rarely face physical threats, our brains will remain on high alert as they search for the potential danger in our lives. Because of this, we often develop a sense of fear around things that cannot actually hurt us ... but which our brains perceive as threats due to the uncomfortable feeling they induce. One such example is embarrassment. The majority of the population is afraid of being embarrassed, even though we logically know that being embarrassed doesn't physically hurt us.

If you truly want to grow as a leader of yourself, you will at some point need to reckon with the fear center of your brain. You will need to challenge your traditional way of thinking and take the "risk" to blossom into who you really are, to explore your potential, and / or to go out on a limb.

You will know when the time is right because you will be feeling a longing or restlessness that you may struggle to name. Listen to that feeling and be brave enough to explore what is next for you on your journey!

Week 37, Day 6

Get Inspired:

"When pride has a hold on our hearts, we lose our independence of the world and deliver our freedoms to the bondage of men's judgement."

-Ezra Taft Benson

Get Aligned:

Pride is another word for ego. Indeed, ego has a powerful silent grip on our choices if we allow it.

Ego is the desire to be seen with favor by other humans. It is a primal trait which we developed in an evolutionary need to be valued by the tribe in our quest for survival. But like many good things, ego can get out of control.

Make a practice of noticing your sense of pride or ego. How and when does it show up? Is it humble, or does it cause you to put up walls around yourself? There is a fine line between the need to have a sense of self-pride, and the counterproductive ego which tells you that it's never your fault if something goes wrong.

The unchecked sense of pride or ego can quickly carry you into a space of "me vs. them". Take actions in your life to be grounded in appreciation and respect for others: volunteer for a civic organization that serves underprivileged individuals, help at an animal shelter, strike up a conversation with a service worker and get to know them, etc. Consider to whom you owe an apology and make it, even if they do not reciprocate. And take credit for not only your successes, but also your mistakes.

Week 36, Day 7

Reflect:

What inspired you this week?

What will you carry forward?

Week 38, Day 1

Get Inspired:

"I expand in abundance, success and love every day as I inspire those around me to do the same."

-Gay Hendricks

Get Aligned:

Gay Hendricks proposes that we have an upper limit, a level of success that we are not comfortable passing, and so we begin unconsciously self-sabotaging when we near it.

I have also heard many great leaders share the sentiment: "Winning is a habit, and losing is a habit".

When we habitually hit a ceiling, we refuse to believe we can pass it. If we can't believe in ourselves, why would anyone else? If you have faced challenges in the past and not found a way forward, you must begin building back your self-belief by creating small "challenges" that you face and overcome. Build in a process for winning on a small scale and grow it as you go.

Do this often enough and you will build a belief in your capabilities that rise to any occasion. We must train our brains, just as an athlete must train for the Olympics.

But this is not the Olympics, this is far more important, this is your LIFE.

It is time to show up with confidence!

Week 38, Day 2

Get Inspired:

"Simply put, confidence trumps IQ in predicting success."

-Katty Kay and Claire Shipman, *The Confidence Code*, Harper Collins Publishers, 2014, pg. 61.

Get Aligned:

Confidence is a home-spun attribute. It is simply the act of believing that we can do something + taking action to achieve an outcome.

The more often we practice believing + action, the more we build our internal confidence.

We don't have to (and shouldn't) rely on others to boost us up. We must find internal reserves so that during the hard times we are able to pull ourselves up and forward.

This is a life-long process of trial, fail, trial again. Eventually we string together some successes, and those are the building blocks of confidence.

Without working to build confidence, you will continuously struggle to be a leader of self. You won't trust your own instincts and capabilities, and you will eventually defer to whatever outside influences surround you.

Week 38, Day 3

Get Inspired:

"There is only one way to get through the fog of fear, and that is to transform it into the clarity of exhilaration."

-Gay Hendricks

Get Aligned:

When we allow fear to takeover, we are stuck in a fog. It is hard to make decisions and to take action.

We can turn it into something positive, however, by committing to a single step forward. You may not know the 'right choice' or 'right action' to take but do something small that feels as though you are moving in a positive direction.

When I first launched my consulting business, I wasn't exactly sure how to price custom programs. I was afraid I would be too high or too low, and both would have negative consequences. As I began to research and talk to trusted advisors... I found a huge variety of pricing. There was no "correct answer". It was scary to quote a potential client; what if I looked like a fool?

But I had to make a choice and stick to it. I learned quickly by client reactions what my sweet spot was, and tweaked pricing for future quotes. Once I practiced (and failed a few times) on my pricing structure, I was able to move forward confidently. That is the power of getting started to lift the fog. The results may not be immediate, but they are powerful.

Week 38, Day 4

Get Inspired:

"Have no fear of perfection; you'll never reach it."

– Marie Curie

Get Aligned:

Perfection is equally motivation and poison for our soul. It drives us to do better, to work harder, and to improve each day. And yet, it holds us back by keeping us fearful, it makes us hesitate least we risk not being ready or perfect, and it demoralizes our confidence.

So how, then, do we find a happy medium between drive and confidence?

If you are afflicted by perfectionism (welcome to the club!), I have come to believe T. Swift was wrong, that we will never truly "shake it off" all the way. But we can learn to challenge it, to push through our comfort zone, and to lessen its grip on us.

For as long as I can remember, and in accordance with the stories from my parents of my childhood, I have been a selective perfectionist for most of my life. That means that when there is something that I personally care about, I am a super-perfectionist about it. And if it's a task or responsibility that means not-so-much to me, I am way more willing to let my efforts be average. This applied to subjects in school that I cared for, job aspects that I preferred, athletics, social endeavors, holiday prep, etc, etc.

One example of this tendency to show up was after our first baby was born, and we had our first nanny ... and I was headed back to work. I had been a mom for only 10 weeks; I was hormonal, nervous, and REALLY wanted to be perfect. I was excited to go back to work, and equally guilty and terrified to leave my baby at home with a nanny. And so, I went into control-freak mode. I had my nanny keep a journal all day of the sleep schedule, feeding schedule, and anything else noteworthy that infants do. Our nanny was wonderful, and luckily got on board to excitedly share the days' details with me. None of this was really necessary, but it made me feel connected to my baby's day as well as gave me a way to feel that I was doing EVERYTHING possible to be a great mom; it allowed me to know her schedule, which in my brain translated to being on top of things and being a prepared mom.

Eventually I had to let go of the obsessive need to be omnipresent. And that *drive-awareness -adjustment* cycle continues even today in all aspects of my life where I tend to lean on perfectionism.

If you are caught in the perfectionist cycle, start with just being aware of its hold on you. From there, consider what tiny adjustments you can make to loosen its grip on your efforts and your mental state. Keep checking in with yourself. As a perfectionist, you probably fear swinging to the other side and becoming lazy. Trust me, that is pretty much impossible for a perfectionist to do!

Relaxing the pressure frees you up to try new things, experiment with creativity, and discover wonderful new capabilities/processes that you never would have considered in the past!

Week 38, Day 5

Get Inspired:

"Childhood is, or has been, or ought to be, the great original adventure, a tale of privation, courage, and constant vigilance, danger, and sometimes Calamity."

-Michael Chabon

Get Aligned:

We begin as creatures destined to explore our world, to try and fail, and then try again. Yet along the way, most of us begin to pull back and scale down our sense of adventure and replace it with fear.

Some individuals (think Sir Richard Branson) have become determined not to live in a space of fear, but to embrace the childlike quality of exploration of 'what could be'. Those are the ones winning at life, as they are not afraid to experience all it has to offer, both highs and lows.

Fear is essential to our growth. Don't work to avoid fear, instead, embrace the notion that fear is merely a collection of butterflies in excitement who are just waiting to be released.

~

Next time you feel fear towards a decision, pause to consider the worst outcome and its likelihood. Challenge yourself to consider the positive potential outcomes. Encourage yourself to release the flurry of butterflies beating in your chest by taking action, just a small step towards this scary thought.

Week 38, Day 6

Get Inspired:

"I have learned over the years that when one's mind is made up, this diminishes fear; knowing what must be done does away with fear."

– Rosa Parks

Get Aligned:

We kidnap ourselves and stay in the realm of insecurity by simply refusing to choose and commit to something. When we get on with the decision making, we can start taking action, and this in turn either leads to a positive result or one that we need to pivot / adjust.

This is what happened to founder and CEO Kendra Scott when launching her self-named jewelry line. "I remember going to the first store and actually being told no and, you know, having the courage to go to another store, finding that inner courage, that perseverance of, 'OK, this one said no, but it's not the end,'" said Scott.

She discovered quickly that the FEAR of "no" or "rejection" was much more powerful when imaging it than in real life. She learned that no was temporary, and to reach her dreams (because her mind was made up), she would just have to keep going. Staying focused on the dream gave her the courage to keep going and look at the empire she now has to show for it!

Week 38, Day 7

Reflect:

What inspired you this week?

What will you carry forward?

Week 39, Day 1

Get Inspired:

"The glory is not in never falling, but in rising every time you fall."

-Chinese Proverb

Get Aligned:

True strength is the ability to fall, dust yourself off, and try again. I'm not suggesting that you should continuously throw yourself against a brick wall. Do not go headlong into worthless pursuits. Instead, scrutinize where you are putting your efforts and evaluate if they remain relevant to your journey. And if they DO matter, if the skill you are trying to master is important … then dust yourself off, analyze what went wrong, adjust, and try again.

Failure is not a source of embarrassment; it is a gift when we learn from it.

Be the example to your children, your peers, those that follow you, and your loved ones. Show Up and Learn.

Week 39, Day 2

Get Inspired:

"Success is not final, failure is not fatal: it is the courage to continue that counts."
— **Winston S. Churchill**

Get Aligned:

Success:

Success comes and goes. We can win one day and be forced to start over the next day. If we judge ourselves only by the "successes" in our lives, we will always be let down. No one can be "successful" all the time. What is an example of a personal success that has come and gone in your life?

Failure:

Failure is also not permanent. It is the process of learning, and if we take our failures and turn them into learning lessons, we propel ourselves towards success. What is an example of a personal failure that has turned into a springboard in your life?

Courage:

Facing failure and pushing forward requires strength. It is comforting to hide after we have slipped … but we will never reach that next success if we succumb to hiding from our failures. What is one thing you will do to learn from a failure and propel yourself forward towards your next success?

Week 39, Day 3

Get Inspired:

"Do one thing every day that scares you."
— Eleanor Roosevelt

Get Aligned:

Just like life-long learning is a habit to keep our mind sharp, doing one "scary" thing each day is a life-long habit that can stretch our comfort zone. It improves our resilience and helps us to turn fear into action. It improves our confidence as we practice trying and not dying. It improves our ability to learn, as we embrace the possibility that failure does not define us.

Look for an opportunity to do one thing each day that scares you; see what transpires for you after a month of learning to be comfortably uncomfortable!

From public speaking to trying sushi to saying no to a friend's request, the options of scary things to try are unique to each of us. Begin to brainstorm some things you can try which seem scary while also encouraging your tiny moments of growth.

Week 39, Day 4

Get Inspired:

"I really think a champion is defined not by their wins but by how they can recover when they fall."

– Serena Williams

Get Aligned:

Can you name a great figure who has not failed? If so, I suggest you wait. We ALL fail at some point, that is the glue that binds us as humans.

If you want to be the champion of your life, you must be willing to try and risk failing. And during the times when you do fail, figure out what went wrong, brush yourself off, and try again while pivoting if needed.

I grew up riding horses and continue to do so. We have a saying in the horse world, it's not IF you will fall, it's WHEN you will fall. We hope that children will fall early in their riding journey so that they can go ahead and get that "fear of falling" out of the way. We celebrate kids when they have their first fall, clapping and encouraging them … and then by giving them a leg up to get back in the saddle immediately. We know falling can be scary, and it does hurt. But if you aren't actually broken, getting back in the saddle immediately is the only way to overcome the fear of "what if".

Will you saddle up in life?

Or will you choose to walk away with the dust of quitting on your jeans?

Week 39, Day 5

Get Inspired:

"Think like a queen. A queen is not afraid to fail. Failure is another steppingstone to greatness."

– Oprah Winfrey

Get Aligned:

Do you allow yourself to think like a Queen (or King)? Have you ever given yourself permission to just go for it, and let the pieces fall where they may?

When we try and fail, these are the stones that lay the pathway forward across the river of life. We can stand at the river's edge, wondering and hoping to get across, or we can start building a path. As we collect our confidence and work to chart our course across the river, we are building bravery. We are making progress. We are putting ourselves out there. We are creating an opportunity for success.

Sure, you may slip and get a wet foot now and again; but isn't it better to have a wet foot while making progress verses standing on the sidelines wondering what is on the other side? What change or excitement will come from staying on only one side of the river?

There is much to explore in this life, we only need to see ourselves as Queens of the expedition and get to the process of living.

Week 39, Day 6

Get Inspired:

"Your best teacher is your last mistake."

-Curtis James Jackson, III

aka: 50Cent

Get Aligned:

The theme is constant and loud when we care to listen. Everywhere we look in life, wise individuals are telling us that mistakes and failures are hidden opportunities.

You can choose to wallow in your frustration over a mistake or take the lesson to heart and use it to your advantage.

Every athlete who has ever found a level of success has learned to use their body in perfect orchestration by taking failures and redirecting their muscles and their mind into a more effective approach.

Every person who has learned to drive a car, to read a book, or to cook a meal has made mistakes.

Do not shy away from the process of learning. It is hard wired deep inside of us and should not be choked out once we reach adulthood. Don't let your ego convince you that it was someone else's fault when you make a mistake. Own the moment and use it to become better.

Learning to fail forward will propel you further along your journey than you can imagine!

Week 39, Day 7

Reflect:

What inspired you this week?

What will you carry forward?

Week 40, Day 1

<u>Get Inspired:</u>

"I've been absolutely terrified every moment of my life — and I've never let it keep me from doing a single thing I wanted to do."

– Georgia O'Keeffe

<u>Get Aligned:</u>

There are three buckets of people that I find when it comes to fear:

1. Those that shrink away from trying new things because of a fear of failure or embarrassment.
2. Those who dabble in facing their fears.
3. Those who laugh in the face of fear, and almost have an insatiable need to always challenge themselves to a higher level.

Where do you fall in this list?

If you are in bucket #1, are you held back from fear of FAILURE or fear of EMBARRASSMENT?

The fear of embarrassment, I find, is rarely acknowledged in adults; and yet, it is highly prevalent. We seem to slip back into our Middle School ways when it comes to risking that moment when our peers may not approve of us. We are told that we should grow out of embarrassment but proves harder to do in real life.

There is a lot to be said for your 40's as you age; that appears to be the decade when a lot of us finally say, *Fuck It*; and we stop caring about others' opinions as much. But it doesn't happen easily for everyone.

One time-tested way to ease the sting of embarrassment? Go about creating small embarrassing moments for yourself on a regular basis. Seriously ... start planning your embarrassing escapades daily.

Drop your bag in a crowded restaurant, let yourself do the snortty laugh in public, raise your hand to ask a question, wear the non-trendy outfit you love, ask your crush on a date, take the yoga class at the gym, admit that you watch the Real Housewives series, dance at your friend's wedding, make a toast at Bob's retirement party, or let people know that you don't like chocolate (OK, this one is weird, I mean, how do you NOT like chocolate?!?).

The point is this, many of those tiny things which you *think* will be embarrassing to admit, say, or do ... will actually fly under the radar and you will be boosting your tolerance of "risky" situations. If you DO become embarrassed in the process, bravo! You are flexing a new muscle and learning that it won't kill you!

Week 40, Day 2

Get Inspired:

"Failure is so important. We speak about success all the time but it is the ability to resist or use failure that often leads to greater success."

– J. K. Rowling

Get Aligned:

What have you failed at today?

If you are not failing, you are likely not pushing out of your comfort zone.

Try for one more push-up, reach out to meet a new person, sing at karaoke night.

Do something that is not guaranteed success.

Leadership requires that we model desirable behaviors. Failing forward is key to success. Showing others when we have failed is not only brave, but necessary for future success.

Show fear that you are stronger than its shackles by leaning into failure as a teacher; this indeed builds strength.

Week 40, Day 3

Get Inspired:

"Gratitude is the gift that always gives back."

-Matthew McConaughey

Get Aligned:

Though we should not be grateful merely as a means to earning something in return, we do by default get back more than we give when we are grateful.

Checkpoint:

How is your gratitude practice going?

If you have fallen off of the wagon, now is a great time to hop back on.

Seriously, stop here and list 5 things you are grateful for. Really breathe them into your soul.

Take these 5 things you are grateful for and share that thought again tomorrow with the Universe.

Do this daily to create a persistent presence of gratitude.

Week 40, Day 4

Get Inspired:

Entropy is the measure of disorder in a system. The **Second Law of Thermodynamics** states that entropy is always increasing because every particle and atomic structure accelerates through time and space.

In nature, the entropy of a system always increases until the system reaches a state of maximum disorder. It should be noted that the rate of entropy increase of some systems is so slow that the increasing disorder is not obvious to the casual observer.

Get Aligned:

What this means is that disorder is all around us and constantly on the rise. Therefore, to manage the disorder in the surrounding universe we must consistently level up our game of focus, intention, and planning. This does not mean that we should strive to control everything around us; but rather to be clear as to where we want to focus our attention and create systems to assist us in that process.

~

We cannot do all things well, all at once. With entropy all around us, we will struggle to do even one thing well if we fail to focus on it. Superstar athletes don't need to be the most naturally talented to be a top performer; instead, they need to be the most committed and most focused.

The same applies in your life. What truly matters to you? Once you answer this question, you should begin to build support systems which allow you to focus your precious resource of attention specifically on these targeted areas.

Want to be CEO? You will need to log the hours with the right people, do the right things, and create the right results to be promoted.

Want to be a professional ballerina? You will need to put in the grueling hours in the studio and beyond to perfect your craft.

Want to get into a specific college? You will have to post the grades, the activities, and the social support that makes you highly qualified to be accepted.

Practice your ability to minimize entropy by focusing on what matters most, and then pay it forward by becoming a mentor to someone else. Apply what you have learned and share those insights and support with someone of the next generation.

Focus is an essential Steppingstone to Success. Honing our ability to focus on that which matters is key to building your presence along Your Own Journey.

Week 40, Day 5

Get Inspired:

Be in the NOW.

"When faced with so many tasks and obligations that you can't figure out which to tackle first, stop. Take a breath. Get present in the moment and ask yourself what is most important this very second – not what's important tomorrow or even an hour from now."

-Greg McKeown, *Essentialism*, Crown Business, 2014, pg. 221.

Get Aligned:

If you are struggling to identify what is the most important, pause to make a list. Consider deadlines and what you *want* versus what you *need* to do. Often, the clarity of seeing it on paper will make your choices easier.

Find a balance:

If you are asked to do something that does not comfortably fit within your timeline, inquire as to the urgency and when it actually needs to be completed. You might be surprised by the answer!

Week 40, Day 6

Get Inspired:

"To be productive in life, we should be focused on a 90day plan AND a 10-year plan at all times. The 2–3-year plans are the quagmire where we get stuck; don't' focus there … that will take care of itself."

-Verne Harnish

Get Aligned:

Know what is urgent and tend to that reality. Know what you are working towards and tend to that garden. The combination of the two will leave you with a pretty clear path along your journey.

Own Your Journey by being intentional with both the 90day and 10year focus. Clarity is king when using it as a lens to make decisions.

The actions required to support your 90day focus will keep you on the path, and passion for the 10year focus will assist in refining your 90day every quarter.

Saying 'no' to the things that do not align with your 90day or 10year vision is a valuable tool for Owning Your Journey. It helps others to see and be able to respect your boundaries.

Week 40, Day 7

<u>Reflect:</u>

What inspired you this week?

What will you carry forward?

Week 41, Day 1

Get Inspired:

"The successful warrior is the average man, with laser-like focus."

-Bruce Lee

Get Aligned:

Focus is the tool that gets you from an idea to action, from average to great, and from passenger to leader.

It is easy to focus on the shiny objects, the loud noises, or the busy tasks (think about how easy it is to get lost in your Instagram feed, reorganizing your desk, or researching that new ergonomic chair). But truly focusing on the big rocks, the strategy, or the detailed execution of a plan is critical as a leader. Be clear on your priorities and create time to concentrate.

Having time for concentrated work does not magically appear. We must protect it on our calendar, create a space that works for us to remain focused, and repeatedly refer to our priorities to maximize the time.

Great leaders-of-self do not squander time. They are deliberate with how they spend their hours in the day. Does this mean you cannot have "down time" or "creative time" as a leader? Absolutely not! In fact, having those relaxed hours of the day are crucial for your long-term wellbeing. By creating dedicated time for deep or focused work, you free up time for more free thinking.

This combination of dedicated focus coupled with intentional space for your brain to relax is the ideal formula for productive leaders of self.

Week 41, Day 2

Get Inspired:

Neuroscientist, **Sarah Shomstein**, from George Washington University, has shared that researchers are finding the act of giving our attention to something creates action. That by simply focusing or thinking about something we want to do/create/experience, we as humans are more likely to follow through and take action towards that direction.

Get Aligned:

By steering our thoughts in a positive manner towards a desired outcome, we are facing the task deliberately. When we choose to do this, we are equipping our brain with a burst of confidence and empowerment that we can deal with the unknown. This supports us in making the choice to take action. And so, once again, we learn that where our attention goes is powerful in creating an outcome. When you string together intention (knowing what outcome you want) with attention (thinking about that outcome) you will be equipped with confidence (the ability to take action).

Focusing on your vision, your mindset, and your presence will lead you to take the right actions which support you're your Own Journey.

Week 41, Day 3

Get Inspired:

Chris Peterson, a positive psychologist, has identified four human responses to adversity through his research:

1. Pathology: People who exhibit significantly reduced social functioning in adversity.
2. Invulnerability: Those who exhibit no major change in their mood when challenged.
3. Resilience: People who bend but don't break when facing a challenge.
4. Personal Growth: Those who grow/thrive in response to danger and adversity.

Get Aligned:

Through my studies and research, I have recognized key abilities in resilient people, which led to crafting this 3-part resilience formula: the combination of Grit, Grace, and Space.

When combined, these three elements ensure that as humans we are more likely to bend, without breaking, in the face of adversity.

Resilience is a learnable skill, and one that each human should embrace. Our work is never done, we must practice regularly to maintain our fitness in this area.

To begin, consider how resilient you feel. Do you seem unbothered by stress, do you thrive under pressure, or do you struggle to make progress when things are tough?

Self-leadership always comes back to awareness of self so that we can make a fitting plan to reach our goals. If you train to develop a resilient presence, you will be well equipped to Own Your Journey.

Week 41, Day 4

<u>Get Inspired:</u>

"For the beauty of the rose we also water the thorns."

-African Proverb

<u>Get Aligned:</u>

Living our Own Journey means we are striving for a beautiful life that resonates with us personally.

It does not protect you from struggles, hard times, or disappointments.

If we are able to reflect on tough situations and learn a lesson, it will help us on our path. If we stay grounded in our belief of our journey and know that we are strong enough to weather the storms, we will find contentment.

Life is a full spectrum of emotions, and we need that rainbow to live in full color. We cannot pick and choose only the pretty moments in life. The painful thorns can serve to support us, as the lessons they offer may bring us insight for future challenges.

~

How we show up in hard times is a testament to who we are. You can feel sad, angry, broken, or scared. But note how you treat others during these moments. Do not take your difficulty out on them. Be brave enough to share that you are in a difficult time and doing your best.

Week 41, Day 5

<u>Get Inspired:</u>

"Grit holds special significance for the achievement of excellence. When you look at the best of the best across domains, the combination of passion and perseverance sustained over the long term is a common denominator."

-Angela Duckworth, *Grit*, Scribner, 2016, pg. 291.

<u>Get Aligned:</u>

When we are able to lean into grit, we are able to rise through adversity and pursue our goals without breaking. As part of the resilience formula, we must be certain to include grit as we strive for our goals. Grit means not giving up when things are hard or uncomfortable, because we know that we can persevere. Grit comes with practice and with belief in oneself.

To improve your grit, start by building daily micro-habits that lead to bigger successes when strung together. Include daily affirmations in your routine. Have a clear vision of what you are trying to accomplish, and of what you cannot change. Track your success and celebrate your growth along the way.

Begin by committing to one or two micro habits and mark a calendar each day that you follow through on these actions. Do not skip a day. This builds your sense of grit and belief that you CAN do hard things. Get an accountability partner who holds you to a higher standard and won't accept your excuses. Grit is a muscle that takes practice to strengthen; get to it.

Week 41, Day 6

Get Inspired:

"There isn't always an easy answer for what is going on – we just take it one day at a time."

-Patrick Underwood

Get Aligned:

Life is tough, and sometimes that is just how it goes. It is never fair. We should strive to embrace and be grateful for the good times and use those to fill up our reserves to be resilient through the hard times.

We will each face difficult situations that come with no direction, no logical reason, and often are laced with heartache. In those moments we must rely on grit to keep putting one foot in front of the other and focus on moving forward. Grit is the ability to collect many tiny grains of sand in pursuit of building that sandcastle.

When we relate our call for grit back to our passionate vision, we have an easier time pressing forward.

Week 41, Day 7

<u>Reflect:</u>

What inspired you this week?

What will you carry forward?

Week 42, Day 1

Get Inspired:

"Excellence does not require perfection."

-Henry James

Get Aligned:

We should all strive to hold ourselves to a standard of grace, not perfection. When we let go of being perfect and instead embrace extending grace to ourselves and others, we will be supporting our practice of resilience. One cannot be resilient and perfect at the same time.

I think of grace as a reset; of taking a damp sponge to a full chalkboard at the end of the day and cleaning it to reveal a blank slate. Grace means you can start fresh, no matter what mistakes you have made. We begin to embrace grace by focusing on the good, by making regular statements of gratitude and acknowledging the positive we are doing or experiencing. We can bolster grace by pausing to consider the intentions behind our actions, and then correcting it going forward as needed. When we journal, we are able to reflect on our days in a less critical manner, and to reveal personal patterns of growth and resilience.

Extending grace to others is an acknowledgement of their human capacity for mistakes. When we accept the positive intent of others, as opposed to focusing solely on the negative outcomes of their choices, we can more freely extend grace.

Week 42, Day 2

Get Inspired:

"I love that this morning's sunrise does not define itself by last night's sunset."

– Steve Maraboli

Get Aligned:

Grace is the ability to wipe our slate clean and start fresh. To give ourselves, and those around us, permission to not be perfect. To know that sometimes our best is not good enough, but that we can try again on a new day.

The fresh arrival of the sun each day is a celebration of new light, new opportunities, and is the epitome of a clean slate.

Let go of what held you down yesterday, look at the world with fresh eyes each day and consider the possibilities. Don't wallow in frustration of the mistakes you've made, but rather learn from them and do better today.

Grace is a key component of the resilience formula. To remain a good leader of self, you must take care to support your resilience, to feed your fire, and to support recovery at the same time.

Week 42, Day 3

Get Inspired:

"Clearings. That is what I needed. Slowly my brain righted itself into spaces unused for months."

-Helen MacDonald

Get Aligned:

Space is a resource highly undervalued.

Space is one component of the Resilience Formula within the Steppingstones of Success.

When we create space to think, to rest, to explore, to play, to create, to consider … we tap into our deepest needs and refill our bucket simultaneously.

Create space both physically and mentally. Find an area where you can be comfortable (indoors or out) and employ an activity that is restorative for you (resting, creating, exercising, or exploring).

Making space for yourself is not selfish, it is self-care and is a crucial piece of self-leadership. Model this for your family and for your teams. Be vocal about where you create space for yourself, and respect when others do so.

Week 42, Day 4

Get Inspired:

"Your sacred space is where you can find yourself again and again."

-Joseph Campbell

Get Aligned:

The final piece of the resilience puzzle is space. Creating space for rest and recovery is the counter point needed for your grit.

As Campbell says, space is that place where you feel most connected to yourself. Be clear on what that space is and create time to indulge yourself there. Create moments of grounding and rest by creating easy access to your space. Don't allow the pollution of distractions while you are in your sacred space. Strive to settle on a rhythm and schedule to visit your space, so that your brain can look forward to its arrival.

"Space" can be a state of mind, a physical space, or an activity that revitalizes you. The only rule is that it truly revives you; it is not an exercise to please anyone else. For many adults this can feel selfish ... but investing in your longevity is never selfish.

Week 42, Day 5

Get Inspired:

"We make a living by what we get, we make a life by what we give."

-Sir Winston Churchill

Get Aligned:

Creating harmony in our lives is the process of finding a comfortable and constant shift between give and take. We can never know true peace or joy if we are not putting good back into the world.

Karma is a force to be respected, it cannot be negotiated with.

When you find you are rolling in abundance, pause to consider how you are sharing that abundance back into the world. That is the key to keeping the cyclical flow ongoing.

Harmony is not equal parts. Harmony is the satisfied state that comes from showing up authentically for Your Own Journey while also putting good back into the world in your own unique way. This keeps the flow of positive energy constantly moving through you and back to you.

Week 42, Day 6

<u>Get Inspired:</u>

"The little things? The little moments? They aren't little."

-Jon Kabat-Zinn

<u>Get Aligned:</u>

Be content in embracing the littlest moments, these are the building blocks that create your life. These are the things you will long for when you are older.

None of us would wish for a few more hours at the computer. We will instead miss the dog that was our faithful companion always at our feet, the sound of our kids singing in the shower down the hall, or the chaos of a full house.

Dream big but soak in the tiny moments and lock them in your heart.

Be certain you aren't excluding the little moments from your life. Participate, be present, and be engaged with your family, your pets, your friends.

As a good leader of self, you must learn to be present and pay attention to the little moments. For this is what matters most!

Week 42, Day 7

Reflect:

What inspired you this week?

What will you carry forward?

Week 43, Day 1

Get Inspired:

"Idleness is not just a vacation, an indulgence or a vice; it is as indispensable to the brain as Vitamin D is to the body, and deprived of it we suffer a mental affliction as disfiguring as rickets ... it is, paradoxically, necessary to getting any work done."

-**Tim Kreider**, *New York Times* essayist

Get Aligned:

To be a good leader of self, and to therefore spearhead your Own Journey, you must incorporate a sense of harmony in your life. Harmony is the give and take remain healthy and feel whole. You cannot push yourself 24-7; there must be time for rest, laziness, and play.

If you are the driven type, you may be at risk of feeling guilty for embracing rest, play, and lazy days. Be certain, however, that this is just as vital as your intense deep work. Create space for "nothing" and allow yourself to be steeped in it.

Be clear with your boundaries. If you are in a space of rest, play, or laziness, communicate to the outside world that you are not available. Use your out of office, turn off your cell, step away from Slack or IM.

PART 4:

Commit to Action

"If there's a book that you want to read, but it hasn't been written yet, then you must write it."

— Toni Morrison

Week 43, Day 2

<u>Get Inspired:</u>

Commitment is defined by *Webster's Dictionary* as:

"An agreement or pledge to do something in the future."

<u>Get Aligned:</u>

A lynch pin in the Self-Leadership Model is the ability to commit with action and mental support to the things which we have identified as important to us. We will not make progress towards Owning Our Journey if we fail to commit to the important things in our lives.

Your commitment, and ensuing support actions, are the pledge to your future self.

Yet, this is the step that I most often see individuals struggling with. It sounds easy in concept but can truly be a challenge to implement.

We have good intentions, but then life starts pulling at us. We are busy with work, with raising a family, and managing our household. We have bright ideas, but worry what the world will think of them, that someone we value will disagree, or even worse, that we will disappoint someone. We want to get started but are overwhelmed by the timeline. We are tired, pulled thin, and scared.

This is the moment that separates great leaders of self from sheep following along with the herd through life.

Be a Lion!

If you *truly* want to Own Your Journey, then you must be brave enough to try. To test your ability by putting forth the effort. By knowing that it might take months or years to reach your goals, and that is ok … because in the end it is really about the journey, not the destination.

Week 43, Day 3

Get Inspired:

As humans, we tend to avoid change. The properties of inertia subliminally leave our brains believing that change is hard.

Inertia comes from **Newton's First Law of Physics** which states that every object will remain at rest or in uniform motion in a straight line unless <u>compelled</u> to change its state by the action of an external force. This tendency to resist changes in a state of motion is inertia. Our aversion to change is therefore a matter of physics.

Get Aligned:

Even though we tend to avoid change, we CAN and should allow ourselves to experience change! Change is uncomfortable but often leads to the best moments of growth in our lives. Consider what is compelling you to make a change; will it have a definite negative impact on your life? If not, maybe you should consider leaning into this external force that is suggesting change either through new motion or through a new path.

Teach your children and/or your teammates that change is a lifelong skillset. Let them see you weigh the options and talk through the benefits of change, even when it is hard.

Change comes when we open ourselves up to a shift in our views and / or our actions.

Week 43, Day 4

Get Inspired:

"You don't make progress by standing on the sidelines whimpering and complaining. You make progress by implementing ideas."

– Shirley Chisholm

Get Aligned:

I have a secret to share ... LIFE IS TOUGH. It is extra tough for some people, and not as tough for others. But one thing is certain, we will all face adversity.

So why do some people rise to the top, seeming to find their way so easily?

They rarely climb easily, there is always a back story that we aren't each privy to. But those people who excel on their journey have a common thread: they don't sit around complaining or feeling sorry for their tough circumstances. They put their boots on one foot at a time and get to doing something about their ideas.

Oprah Winfrey is a wonderful example of this. She grew up in poverty to a single teenaged mother, was abused, and herself became pregnant at the age of 14 (losing her son after complications of premature birth). After losing the baby, she was sent to Tennessee to live with her father, where she earned a job on a radio station. From there, she went on to college to study broadcasting, was hired by a local news channel, ended up taking over their morning show, and then came The Oprah Winfrey Show and the rest of her dazzling success that we all see.

Oprah chose to focus on doing something with her life, as opposed to complaining about the undoubtedly tough situations she faced. She had ideas and approached them with authenticity, determined to do something with those ideas.

Consider what ideas may be buried within you beneath a pre-occupation with complaining. Pull those forward and see what begins to happen in your life!

Choose to be the Captain of your ship, not a victim of the tide.

Week 43, Day 5

Get Inspired:

"All big things come from small beginnings. The seed of every habit is a single, tiny decision. But as that decision is repeated, a habit sprouts and grows stronger. Roots entrench themselves and branches grow. The task of breaking a bad habit is like uprooting a powerful oak within us. And the task of building a good habit is like cultivating a delicate flower one day at a time."

-James Clear

As quoted from: Clear, James. *Atomic Habits: Tiny Changes, Remarkable Results: An Easy & Proven Way to Build Good Habits & Break Bad Ones*. New York, New York, Avery, an imprint of Penguin Random House, 2018.

Get Aligned:

Do you remember the experiment in pre-school that involved a Ziploc bag, a small amount of soil, one seed, and a few drops of water? You plant the seed (usually some sort of bean) in the bag of soil, zip it up, and the teacher tapes each person's bag to the window. For weeks you would wait and watch for signs of growth. Finally, you would see the sprouts appear and before you knew it there was a bean plant creeping to the top of the bag. My children both loved this experiment during their preschool years, and it was often requested to be repeated at home. This is because watching the transformation is incredibly rewarding, after you endure the waiting period.

Try this with yourself. Commit to a tiny habit and put it on display so that you see it daily. If you want to get into shape, start with a 10-minute walk or run each day. Track it on a calendar that remains visible for you to see the progress you are making. Add a little time each week as you grow in strength.

Before you know it, you will be feeling stronger, breathing better, and you will find that the habit is on autopilot. *I prefer to workout in our home gym vs. going to a gym. However, I admit it is easy to get off-track, miss a day, or cut workouts short. To combat this, a year or so ago I bought an inexpensive dry erase calendar to hang in the gym. Now, I track what I do each day (and the time spent) so that at the end of each week I have a visual reminder of what I have achieved ... and some motivation to keep it going.

If you are trying to rid yourself of a bad habit, begin by trying to re-direct or replace that habit with a newer more positive habit. For example, if you are struggling to speak kindly to yourself it is nearly impossible to erase that habit by admonishing yourself when it happens. Instead, as you feel it beginning to happen, redirect yourself to say something positive about your abilities or future. If you slip into the negative don't fret, simply continue adding 1-2 positive statements for each negative one that slips out. Eventually the positive statements will choke out the negative ones and you will be left with a more productive habit!

I had an Aunt growing up who wanted to quit smoking; after years of smoking, she knew that it was as much a habit for her *hands to be busy* as it was about the smoking itself. To stick with the transition, she picked up quilting. It kept both of her hands busy, she quit smoking, and she picked up a new hobby along the way!

Week 43, Day 6

Get Inspired:

"Dig deep within yourself, for there is a fountain of goodness ever ready to flow if you will keep digging."

-**Marcus Aurelius**, *Mediations*, 7.59

Get Aligned:

Whenever you are thinking of giving up or quitting, consider if you have a deeper well of reserves to tap into.

Our personal energy is rechargeable if we don't deplete it. When we continue to care for ourselves, we will be able to tap into that natural resource. However, if we neglect to care for ourselves then the well will eventually run dry.

Find consistent ways to protect and replenish your natural resource of energy. No one else will do this for you, we must each be masters of our own well.

As you pursue Your Own Journey, it is imperative that you find and manage your energy sources in a manner that allows you the strength to maintain forward and positive thoughtful actions in life.

Week 43, Day 7

Reflect:

What inspired you this week?

What will you carry forward?

Week 44, Day 1

Get Inspired:

"Think Less. Take Action. Be Authentic."

-Katty Kay and Claire Shipman

Get Aligned:

In their tremendous book, *The Confidence Code*, Kay and Shipman detail the many tiny details that combine to build or erode one's confidence. This quote is their summation of advice to improve your confidence. The simplicity in this quote means that each of us can readily apply it and boost our confidence over time, though it does take discipline and awareness to embrace these three steps.

Think Less:

Be willing to let go of that drive to overanalyze each thought in your head or situation that you face.

Take Action:

Action is the anecdote to fear. Put your body into motion with a plan or physical action which has you stepping up to face your fear and work through it.

Be Authentic:

Stop trying to be or immolate someone else. It doesn't matter if they are "amazing", you are not them and never will be. Be your true self and let that brand become one worth knowing.

Week 44, Day 2

Get Inspired:

"It is never too late to be what you might have been."

— George Eliot

Get Aligned:

Each day is a new opportunity to begin again. We have a fresh start and can begin taking the small steps required to move in a direction that we desire. It is only too late if we refuse to acknowledge or make an effort towards who we want to be.

If you were nasty or impatient to a colleague, your spouse, or your child yesterday, say you are sorry and show up in a more compassionate form today.

If you are lagging on your wellness routine, start today with some form of exercise, meditation, and/or healthy nutrition.

If you haven't gotten that promotion at work, start today by asking a mentor/manager what you need to do to prepare, and then begin.

If you want to build something of your own or travel the world, start your savings account today.

Whatever you do, don't waste another day thinking of what you COULD have done; take action.

Week 44, Day 3

Get Inspired:

"You only live once, but if you do it right, once is enough."

— Mae West

Get Aligned:

Passion is available to each of us. And passion is what makes your journey memorable in a palpable way. Have you ever sat with an elderly person and listened to their stories? You can see the passion of a memory light up their eyes and ignite sparks of joy.

We should all want to have memories and stories of great passion tucked away in our brains. However, this can only happen if we are brave enough to take a few calculated risks and go with passion towards our goals.

We don't get a "do-over". Each of us will eventually run out of time, so make the most of it by living in a way that fills your heart and soul. Screw the critics; instead listen to your own True North and remain loyal to Your Own Journey by taking action to live in your truth.

Week 44, Day 4

Get Inspired:

"Cumulatively small decisions, choices, actions, make a very big difference."

-Jane Goodall

Get Aligned:

At times it can feel as though our small actions are worthless. Why even try taking a few steps when the mountain we must climb is so large?

If you have ever been hiking up the side of a mountain (no matter how big or small), you will know that looking up, especially when you begin to feel tired, can be disarming. However, focusing on putting one foot in front of the other is doable and reduces that feeling of impossibility.

When we make small choices each day to make tiny thoughtful actions, they string together to create a much stronger outcome than if we only provide one strong burst of energy. Stay the course, know where you want to go, and keep taking those small steps to get there. That is how you Own Your Journey one step at a time.

Week 44, Day 5

<u>Get Inspired:</u>

The purpose of criticism is to help others improve. The purpose of praise is to help others know what to keep doing more of."

-**Kim Scott**, *How to Be Awesome at Your Job*, episode 150

<u>Get Aligned:</u>

Criticism without notes of HOW to improve is hurtful. Praise without linking it to specific behaviors is wasteful.

~

In the process of improving your personal operating system, be very clear with your personal reviews:

What don't you like about how you function right now, and why not?

What type of shift (behavior, focus, or mindset) would make you feel as though you are truly Owning Your Journey?

What are you doing well lately?

Why does this behavior serve you and how does it align with your overall goals? What positive outcome is it supporting?

~

How we speak to ourselves MATTERS. If we only offer negative thoughts and criticism to ourselves, it becomes exhausting, and we crush our spirit. When we offer empty positive thoughts without supporting specific behaviors or mindsets, we don't know how to keep that momentum going.

Offer yourself both criticism AND praise. Treat yourself like someone you love.

Week 44, Day 6

Get Inspired:

"Vision without execution is hallucination."

-Thomas Edison

Get Aligned:

Thomas Edison was an epic failure.

He tried and failed more often than the average man, and THAT is what made him so successful! He knew how to surround himself with the right people who could fill in the gaps for his weaknesses, who could financially support his creativity and vision, and who would allow him to try and fail as he worked towards his goals.

He didn't limit the possibility of bringing his visions to life by trying to do it all on his own; he knew he would give up or fall short. And so, he put the plan in place to support the execution of his ideas.

We, too, must recognize where we will fall short or need support along Our Journey. We should plan to cultivate a team or tribe of the right people who will help us as we pursue our vision with thoughtful action. That can be cheerleaders, brain power, physical strength, persuasive communicators, financial backers, or a long list of other supporters.

Don't let your vision turn cold by failing to execute on it. Make the tough choices and go get the help you need.

Begin now by outlining what support or help you will need as you pursue your vision and begin to brainstorm names of people that fit those roles.

Week 44, Day 7

Reflect:

What inspired you this week?

What will you carry forward?

Week 45, Day 1

Get Inspired:

A study on sleep, published in 2010, found that too few hours of sleep each night resulted in increased risk for early death.

-Cappuccio

Cappuccio FP; D'Elia L; Strazzullo P; Miller MA. "Sleep duration and all-cause mortality: a systematic review and meta-analysis of prospective studies." *SLEEP* 2010;33(5):585-592.

Get Aligned:

Protecting our sleep is essential for recovery and repair. It reduces our stress hormones and restores a sense of calm.

Be strict with your bedtime. Honor the vessel that carries you day to day and invest in the long-term abilities of both your brain and your heart by getting the recommended 7-9 hours of sleep each night.

*PS- if you are a parent of young babies, obviously this is impossible. Just know, your day will come when you can return to a somewhat normal sleep pattern. Until then, hang in there ... you are doing great!

~

Taking care of oneself is essential to be able to function as a leader at the highest level. Exhaustion is not a badge of honor; it is a sign of disrespect to your own body.

Week 45, Day 2

Get Inspired:

"But what does Socrates say? 'Just as one person delights in improving his farm, and another his horse, so I delight in attending to my own improvement day by day.'"

-**Epictetus**, *Discourses*, 3.5.14

Get Aligned:

Epictetus is encouraging us to spend a little time each day improving ourselves. When we were children, this was expected of us. We went to school, we explored our worlds, we practiced sports. And then we grew up and got jobs.

But our job of learning and growing is never complete. Do one thing each day that is a practice in growth. You won't regret the time you spend investing in yourself.

Get a growth buddy; someone who also values the concept of learning or challenging themselves in a new way. Read new books together, practice a new sport together, or debate politics as you consider their implications on our world. Anything to stretch and grow as a human.

The action of challenging yourself will lead to new discoveries along Your Journey.

Week 45, Day 3

Get Inspired:

Consider '**The Deep work Hypothesis**' from Cal Newport

"The ability to perform deep work is becoming increasingly rare at the exact same time it is becoming increasingly valuable in our economy. As a consequence, the few who cultivate this skill, and then make it the core of the working life, will thrive."

-Cal Newport, *Deep Work: Rules for Focused Success in a Distracted World*, Grand Central Publishing, 2016, pg. 14.

Get Aligned:

Life is loud and busy. There are infinite distractions pulling for your attention at every moment, and we have been conditioned to toggle back and forth between these forces all day at a rapid pace.

If we commit to creating time and space for deep uninterrupted work, we will have an advantage that allows us to pursue our passions at a deeper level, and with more productive outcomes.

To begin, consider where you can block your calendar just once each week for 3-4 hours of deep work. It may sound absurd or overwhelming, but if you commit to the process, the outcomes of what you accomplish are astounding.

Please note, this is not an overnight transition. You will flounder at first as you learn how to dig deep within your deep-work zone but keep trying.

Bonus Tip:

Deep work marries nicely with Covey's concept of "First Things First" as it is a pro-active, not reactive approach to work.

~

Creating a protected space to carry out the actions (or work) required to support your vision is essential to the process of Owning Your Journey.

Week 45, Day 4

<u>Get Inspired:</u>

"The bad news is that time flies. The good news is you're the pilot."

-Michael Altshuler

<u>Get Aligned:</u>

Be master of your time, and you will always have enough of it. The concept of abundance also applies to your time. We all have the same amount of it, but we can choose to feel as though its "not enough" or "just right".

It becomes easier to be comfortable with time when we know how we are spending it, and why.

Begin by tracking your time all day every day for 7 days. Track your sleep, internet surfing, work, commuting, errand running, chores, tv watching, exercising, social media, and all of the things in-between.

You may be surprised with the results. Most of us have a lot of wasted time created by toggling back and forth between tasks, or time wasted by not focusing when necessary.

Clear the clutter, hire help where you can, and protect your important buckets such as deep work, family, wellness, and sleep.

Select one area of wasted or inefficient time on your calendar and make a change to impact it. This may be something seemingly small and inconsequential; but time regained is just likes grains of sand … compounded together they can fill a vast ocean!

Week 45, Day 5

Get Inspired:

"How we spend our days is, of course, how we spend our lives."

-Annie Dillard

Get Aligned:

Are you spending your time in a way that aligns with the goals of your life?

If not, you are setting yourself up for disappointment.

You are the only one who has the power to change how you spend your time. Maybe it's a tiny shift like less time with TV and more time playing games with family/friends. Maybe it's a massive shift to a new job that lets you work remotely and cuts down the hours spent commuting back and forth to the office.

Only you can decide, and only you can execute on this plan.

How you spend your time is an action that sends a clear message about your priorities to everyone around you. Be sure it aligns with your intended message.

If you say that being a present and engaged parent is a top priority for you, yet you rarely make it to your children's activities or even home for dinner, then your intentions and actions are not aligned. It's time for a change to one or the other.

Week 45, Day 6

Get Inspired:

"Leaders with good problem-solving ability demonstrate five qualities:

They anticipate problems … They accept the truth … They see the big picture … They handle one thing at a time … They don't give up a major goal when they're down."

--John C. Maxwell, *21 Indispensable Qualities of a Leader*, Thomas Nelson Publishers, 1999, pg.98-100.

Get Aligned:

Being able to solve problems is essential as a leader of teams, of your family, and of yourself. Let's explore a few real-life scenarios of how you can level up your problem-solving capabilities in all areas of life:

1. Anticipate the Problems:

As a mother of 2 kids who play multiple sports throughout the year, I have learned as their leader to anticipate problems. My mom-mobile stays stocked throughout the year with key elements to solve for problems that will inevitably arise. My cargo area is always loaded with the following items: Bottled water (I always keep a 12pack in the car because you never know when they will run out). First Aide Kit with instant icepacks (used more times than I care to mention). Rain Gear (jackets, hats, umbrellas). Blankets (specifically, warm ones and waterproof ones). Snacks (anything that I can keep on hand for a quick pick-me up). Seasonal Support (sunscreen, bug spray, hot hands, etc.). Hats (ball caps, winter beanies, and gloves, too). Coat (and extra coat is always on hand for random weather). Slides (cheap flip flops to get kids out of cleats if we need to run errands after games). Activity Pack (coloring books, cards, Rubix cube, Simon, etc. ... things to entertain the sibling who is stuck waiting).

2. Accept the Truth:

I have a client, "Laura" who recently had to face a hard truth: her growing company had outgrown the capabilities of a valued employee. She knew, liked, and trusted this employee; but the needs of the role had outpaced the growth of the individual. Instead of continuing to spend money on a lost cause, Laura had an honest meeting with the employee to discuss if there were other appropriate roles for her internally, and to offer the gift of a career coach to support this individual in exploring options outside of the company.

3. See the Big Picture:

"Nathan", a friend of mine, was busy building out his sales team. He had the unique situation of being able to hire seven out of the ten reps within a one-year period. He was able to think big picture; he needed to fill the bench with both solid rock stars who wanted to stay long term, rising stars who would eventually move on, and budding professionals who would fall in behind the rising stars. He was also interested in hiring for personalities that would complement and challenge each other, as well as reps with diverse backgrounds to share their learned experiences from a variety of industries and technical expertise. It took Nathan 14 months to build this ideal team. But, armed with his big picture vision, he was able to create a powerhouse team that went on to be top performing year after year.

4. Handle One Thing at a Time:

"Lindsey", a coaching client of mine, was graduating from her doctoral program, which happened to be overseas. In the months leading up to her graduation, we spoke often of her desires for formal work placement, preparing for final examinations, sitting for boards, her need to secure living space, the logistics of moving back to the States, and the process of interviewing. The sheer volume of "responsibilities" that were crashing down on her in a rainstorm after four years of a grueling but steady program, was overwhelming. When she would start to consider ALL the big decisions at once, she would understandably become frustrated and anxious. Lindsey learned to tackle one thing at a time and worked hard not to get caught up in the long to-do list. At this pace, she was able to accomplish SO MANY big choices and processes, in a small amount of time, with much less stress.

5. Don't Give Up a Major Goal when you are Down:

Tragedy struck like lightning for my client "Elle". In an instant, she lost her partner to a heart attack, and was left to pick up the pieces. She lost her home, her plans for their pending retirement together, her best friend, and her source of passion. As a business owner, she was responsible for keeping the lights on for many employees. In addition to the mere devastation of logistics and plans, Elle's heart was shattered into a million pieces that she was struggling to put back together. But she persevered. She found outlets for her grief, and invited moments of joy back into her life. She kept her business afloat and made a new home. She didn't just survive, she reached back into her files and resurrected old goals of writing and photography. She allowed her grief to exist but did not give up along the way; instead, she put effort into these goals and began making impressive progress on rekindling the creative light inside of her.

We all face tragedy, loss, challenge, and uncertainty at points in our lives. Learning to problem solve will help you navigate these moments as an effective leader. Acting in a thoughtful manner means you are Owning Your Journey verses being a passenger on the river of life.

Week 45, Day 7

Reflect:

What inspired you this week?

What will you carry forward?

Week 46, Day 1

Get Inspired:

"Persist, pivot, or concede. It's up to us, our choice every time."
— **Matthew McConaughey**

Get Aligned:

Like Kenny Rogers said, "*Know when to hold 'em, know when to fold 'em, know when to walk away, know when to run*". This is one of the toughest questions in life: **When do we shift?**

It will be a personal question every time, and only you can answer it. You will often have a choice to persist, pivot, or walk away. Be sure that you can live with the consequences of the choices you make.

How will you act in the face of a challenge?

Do you default to digging your heels in, walking away, or pivoting in the face of challenge? Consider the message this action is sending to the world.

Could you be more open to shifting or walking away next time? Could you find the strength to dig in and persist a bit longer next time? What would this mean to Your Own Journey and the people around you?

Week 46, Day 2

Get Inspired:

"Nature is restorative because it frees up the top-down part of your brain in a way that allows it to recover… Nature has this not totally unique but more powerful ability to capture your attention in a different way. Evolutionarily, nature is a powerful bottom-up experience for us."

-Adam Gazzaley

Get Aligned:

If you are feeling broken down, stressed, or simply out of sorts, consider some time in Nature as your remedy. Science backs up the notion that nature heals. And while it is not the only option to experience that top-down brain relaxation, it is surely an accessible one. Bonus affect, a study published in *PLoS ONE*, authored by neuroscientist Dave Strayer, found that individuals had a 50% improvement in creativity after just a few days in nature.

~

Relax your brain and boost your creativity in the process by planning a 3-day hiking or camping trip with trusted friends or relatives. Want to get these impacts for your office team? Plan an experiential nature-based team-building offsite meeting. It may feel awkward or uncomfortable at first, but you will see the direct impact on your team's ability to communicate, connect, and create new ideas!

~

As a good leader of self, you are focused on taking action to achieve your goals and visions. But you must also own the action needed to restore your mind, body, and soul. You must create space for rest and recovery, and to boost your creative thoughts, so that you support and feed the process of knowing your vision.

Week 46, Day 3

Get Inspired:

The Power of Walking

Walking may be the most overlooked and underappreciated tool available to our brains, our motivation, and our ability to take action. Consider these thought leaders' reflections:

"When we walk, we naturally go to the fields and woods: what would become of us, if we walked only in a garden or a mall?"

-Henry David Thoreau

"[Walking is] the best way to go more slowly than any other method that has ever been found."

-Frederic Gros

"All truly great thoughts are conceived while walking."

-Nietzsche

Get Aligned:

Follow the great minds of those above, and others such as Aristotle and St Augustine of Hippo:

Explore the concept of *solvitur ambulando* (in walking it will be solved).

Simply put, when we allow our bodies to move in a non-taxing way (such as walking), we ignite our brain.

Make walking part of your daily ritual. I did many years ago and there is not a more restorative practice in my day than that of walking. Do this before sunrise, during a conference call, with the kids and/or dog in the evening, or simply for five minutes a few times a day to stretch your legs.

Stick with it for three weeks, and then notice the impact it has on your entire being:

Do you feel more relaxed and/or more energized?

Do you find your thoughts flow freely while walking?

Does walking wake your inner curiosity?

Do you find a state of meditation while walking?

~

The action of walking will feed your vision, your mindset, and your presence.

Of note, I realize that not every human is blessed with the capability to walk. For those whom walking is not available to, I encourage you to find a modified movement outdoors. You will reap the same benefits as walking!

Week 46, Day 4

Get Inspired:

"Strategy is about making choices, trade-offs. It's about deliberately choosing to be different."

-Michael Porter

Get Aligned:

In business, there comes a time that we must move from reactive to strategic if we wish to grow in our career path. The same goes for your personal life.

Strategy means we are clearly considering our options, and making a choice that best aligns with our goals/needs/values. We are making a choice, and in doing so we often give up something. Saying "no" to options can feel scary because we are afraid to give it away. This intentional choice, however, will free you in the long run to move forward with action, intention, and focus.

Be brave enough to make a choice and pass on opportunities that aren't a good fit. The right opportunity at the wrong time is still the wrong opportunity.

As you pass on options that "don't fit", be confident enough to share that wisdom or train of thought with others.

Week 46, Day 5

Get Inspired:

"With self-discipline, all things are possible. Without it, even the simplest goal can seem like an impossible dream."

-Theodore Roosevelt

Get Aligned:

And this is the root of it all…

When we are children, we rely on our parents to create boundaries and rules for us so that we can learn and grow in a safe manner. As adults, sometimes we struggle to create our own boundaries, rules, or positive habits.

If you seem to always have "good ideas" or "good intentions" that never quite come to life, you are likely struggling with discipline.

Despite what social media will have you believe, there is no easy way, no overnight success. There is only dedication and not giving up which leads to success (and a lot of failures along the way).

If you truly want to accomplish something, you must figure out how to stay committed to the process of getting there.

Want to maintain a healthy body weight? You must create DAILY healthy habits, not for the short term but for the long term.

Want to learn a foreign language? You must practice daily.

Want to become the boss? You must show up with a willing attitude, focused approach, and the commitment to be great at your work.

Find a way to set small realistic habits (micro-habits) which you can easily implement in your life. Slowly add to those as you build a stronger base.

Stop making excuses and hold yourself accountable, or nothing will change.

~

Put your money where your mouth is. Create a family challenge to hold yourselves accountable for a new habit or goal. Each night as a family, ask about your individual progress. Anyone who has not held themselves accountable shall contribute to the family money jar (to be donated to charity).

Another way to expand the impact of accountability is to find an accountability partner; someone with whom you check-in and share your results. This can be a friend who is also looking to improve their self-leadership, or a coach whom you hire. Both works, but I find that folks who struggle to keep their promises to themselves do best when they are investing in a coach. This transfer of money puts more pressure on them to follow through so that it is money well spent.

Week 46, Day 6

Get Inspired:

"Busyness as Proxy for Productivity: In the absence of clear indicators of what it means to be productive and valuable in their jobs, many knowledge workers turn back toward an industrial indicator of productivity: doing lots of stuff in a visible manner."

- Cal Newport, *Deep Work: Rules for Focused Success in a Distracted World*, Grand Central Publishing, 2016, pg. 64.

Get Aligned:

Busy is bullshit.

Busy is often still used as a badge of honor, even though it plays no valuable role in our lives today. As knowledge workers, busy has no bearing on your productivity. As a parent, being busy does not make you more attentive to your child. As a friend, being busy does not make you more loyal.

Don't get caught in the "busyness trap". That space that *feels* like we are doing important things because of our schedule (both professionally and personally).

We don't have to be busy to be productive. We can instead choose to be focused and get our work done in a deep and thoughtful manner by taking away distractions and transitions, which in turn frees us up for more relaxed or creative time.

To be a true leader of self, you must manage your time and your focus.

Catch yourself in the act of being "busy"; stop and determine if it is productive or merely a habit. Choose to be more intentional about your time, and others will observe the shift in your patterns.

Week 46, Day 7

<u>Reflect:</u>

What inspired you this week?

What will you carry forward?

Week 47, Day 1

Get Inspired:

"Habits are the compound interest of self-improvement."

-James Clear

Get Aligned:

Each time we invest our efforts into a small habit, we are reinforcing that it matters to us. It's like making an automatic small contribution to our savings account on a daily or weekly basis, and one day that account has reached thousands of dollars.

Examples of 5 routine habits that pay off big-time in the long run:

1. **Get up when your alarm goes off.** Avoid the trap of hitting snooze 2-3 times and losing that extra 20minutes in your day. Either plan to sleep an extra 20minutes, or plan to get up. Get rid of the grey area. If you really like the feeling of hitting snooze, purposefully set your alarm for 5-10 minutes earlier than your desired get-up time, hit the snooze once, and still have feet on the floor at your pre-determined time.

2. **Meal planning.** Take 20-30minutes once a week to plan out your meals for the week and make a corresponding grocery list or restaurant reservations.

This will keep you from those last-minute binges and unexpected splurges that may upset your waistline, your hangry kids, and your budget.

3. **Have a movement routine - and stick to it.** Fitness will never happen if you hope to have time for it. Put time on your calendar every day, just as you schedule other meetings or picking up your children from daycare. You don't have to be a slave to the gym to be healthy! Find something you like (or don't hate): walking, cycling, running, stretching, gardening, Tai Chi, etc. These are all easy to do at home with little to no monetary investment. Consistent movement is the one thing we can all do to extend our lives.

4. **Save your money**. We all live on different budgets with different financial responsibilities and goals. But, in life, most of us will need access to that "bonus" money we have saved. If you are reading this book, you are most likely able to afford to sock away just a little bit of money each month. If you are new to this, start with an auto transfer of just $5 per week into your savings account. Slowly build and increase the amount to a level that feels comfortable for you. Create your own safety net in life; no one else owes this to you.

5. **Gratitude statements**. Create time each day to express gratitude, appreciation, and/or joy. This can be through prayer, song, journaling, family discussions, or simply through repeating a gratitude statement in your mind. This is best achieved if you set aside a specific

time of day and make it part of your routine. I like to think about mine while I fall asleep at night; it calms my mind and puts it into a restful and relaxed state for sleeping.

~

Steal from this list of highly effective micro-habits or create your own. Finding clarity on your "basic" habits and sticking to them will be an investment in your future.

Week 47, Day 2

Get Inspired:

"If there is a way into the woods there is also a way out."

-Irish Proverb

Get Aligned:

If you can find your way into trouble, you can find your way out. And let's be honest, we ALL find our way into trouble at some point in our lives!

The trick is to be honest, own your mistakes, and create a plan to rectify where you went wrong. It will likely hurt, take time, and generally feel exhausting. But this is how you will free yourself.

Drinking too much? Deal with it, getting professional help if you need it.

Having an affair? Stop being so selfish and start being honest.

Failing to follow through on a commitment? Stop what you are doing, cut the fat, and reset your commitments to focus on what matters.

Racking up debt you can't afford? Stop spending and create a recovery plan.

There is never shame in the process of improving yourself. There is, however, shame in hiding from reality. If you plan to Own Your Journey, you must own all aspects of it … even the bits where you have made a mistake or a wrong turn.

~

Be prepared to offer help and support to people you care about if they are stuck in the woods … but be prepared and at peace with the reality that not everyone is ready to accept help.

Week 47, Day 3

Get Inspired:

"There is absolutely no innovation without failure."

- Brené Brown

Get Aligned:

Failure is something that most of us try to avoid. But the reality is that failure is necessary for improvement and growth.

Our brains are wired to be puzzle solvers, that is one of our greatest strengths as homo sapiens. We are naturally curious, and our species has survived and thrived in large part due to our puzzle solving nature. It has taken centuries of failures to get us to where we are today.

Flip the script, instead of considering failure as a negative try to frame it in a new light. Failure is the process of learning one way that doesn't work and leads you closer to your answer. We should indeed celebrate failing as a means of moving closer to our target.

Failure is only bad when we let it hold us back or steep fear into our hearts.

Take action and see what happens. Turn failures into clues of how to do better the next time.

Week 47, Day 4

Get Inspired:

"You must gain control over your money, or the lack of it will forever control you."

-Dave Ramsey

Get Aligned:

If you are afraid of it, it can be painful to take a real look at your money. Start by knowing where you are. Take stock of your finances and understand what you have and what you owe. Get real on areas where you need to cut back, invest, share, and grow.

This snapshot is not a judgement against you. It is merely a reality check so that you can plan to live with more financial health.

As you make your financial plans, be sure to include giving into your budget. Even if you are in extreme debt, committing even $2 each month to a favorite charity sets the tone for abundance and shared wealth in the universe.

This action reinforces the visions you have for financial stability in life and an abundant mindset around money. Small actions to support your financial stability build your confident presence for managing your personal wealth. Invest in your future by building positive financial habits.

Week 47, Day 5

Get Inspired:

"You will never plow a field by turning it over in your mind."

-Irish Proverb

Get Aligned:

Action begets action.

When we ruminate about a problem or a challenge we are faced with, we often get nowhere fast. When we consider our choices and then take a step in any direction, we are much more likely to land at a productive outcome.

Get your hands dirty, start doing the work and stop planning. Stop hiding behind the process of "research" or "consideration" or "investigation". Just start doing.

Early in my career, upon my first promotion to manager, I was working diligently to prepare for a massive presentation to the team. I kept re-working it and was overanalyzing every detail. Eventually, my manager kindly reminded me that I had to trust myself and just get started! He said there were going to be imperfect portions because I was human but learning and fixing as I went was far superior to waiting as I continued to revise and revisit the same information in a ruminative fashion.

His advice still rings clear and powerful in my head. As I go to publish this book, I know there will be imperfect parts, despite the best efforts in my writing and outside editing. At some point, we must let go of perfection and instead aim for action if we want to make progress.

Week 47, Day 6

Get Inspired:

"Life is a great big canvas, and you should throw all the paint on it you can."

– Danny Kaye

Get Aligned:

What a beautiful visual this quote provides! Imagine, having no restrictions or fear of "getting it wrong", and just throwing paint all over a giant canvas. This would indeed be a freeing exercise.

Why then do we not treat life like this? Why do we select one lane and believe we have to stay in it? Why do we not give ourselves permission to live with passion and to explore all the colors or patterns that interest us?

Humans are multi-dimensional creatures with complex brains. To maintain our evolvement, we must continue to pique our curiosity and explore our creativity. Without those habits, we will wither on the vine.

Learn to explore your ideas, and also to actively experience different colors in life.

If you are the leader of a team, a family, or other group … consider how you encourage them to "play with paint". Are you making opportunities for employees to explore and learn new skills? Are you encouraging your kids to try different sports, instruments, or forms of art? Are you helping your philanthropic group to consider new ways to engage supporters?

Step outside of the lines and allow your ideas to blossom. Just because you think it, doesn't mean you have to act on it!

Week 47, Day 7

Reflect:

What inspired you this week?

What will you carry forward?

Week 48, Day 1

Get Inspired:

"For every reason it's not possible, there are hundreds of people who have faced the same circumstances and succeeded."

– Jack Canfield

Get Aligned:

It is often said that the thing which is the deciding factor if an entrepreneur will succeed or fail, is how long they are willing to stick with it. In other words, by giving up we kill the dream; by sticking with it we find new ways to create success.

If you find yourself making excuses for why you can't follow your passion, ask that special someone on a date, learn a new skill, leave a crappy marriage, or go back to school, etc., etc., etc.... it is time for some personal tough love.

What are you truly afraid of? Explore the worst-case scenario and challenge yourself to decide if it truly is life-limiting.

What would happen if you DID push through to try for a specific outcome? Explore the possible outcomes of sticking with it. Consider what your daily life would feel like while trying to get from point A to point B, what the outcomes might be, who your supporters and naysayers will be, and how you will feel when you do push through the obstacle.

Are you spending the time and effort to plan, prepare, and dream of a goal, only to stop short when it comes time to act?

Start holding yourself accountable for the action that will produce the results you desire. Get clear on your KPIs (Key Performance Indicators); these are the small actions that add up to big results. I learned early in my career as a sales professional that KPIs are essential to long-term results, even though many of them feel "annoying". They are so essential, in fact, that as a business owner I track my professional KPIs weekly! To meet my personal health goals, you guessed it, I also track the KPIs which are essential to my long-term wellbeing.

Be accountable.

Be brave.

Make a choice and execute with focus.

Week 48, Day 2

Get Inspired:

"A vision is not just a picture of what could be; it is an appeal to our better selves, a call to become something more."

-Rosabeth Moss Kanter

Get Aligned:

Trying to Own Your Journey by cultivating a strong sense of self leadership requires that you have a vision. It does not have to be a life-altering, gut-punching change ... but it does need to be something that inspires you and guides you like a light forward.

Without this light, you risk wandering aimlessly, or worse, falling for any path or idea that others share with you. Joining others on a path they have presented is not necessarily a bad thing, but it is counterproductive if it lays in opposition to your own True North. If you don't take the time to discover and know your True North, you will lack the vision for how you want to live and show up, especially when things are difficult.

A vision is a call to action.

Answering that call is the process of making your way down your path of discovery and success.

Week 48, Day 3

Get Inspired:

"Doing nothing gets you nothing."

– Sean Reichle

Get Aligned:

Indecision is one of the most dangerous adversaries in our lives. When we give our power over to indecision, we are destined to sit in a purgatory of our own making.

When you have a goal or a dream, it will absolutely not come true if you do nothing to pursue it. If you are in a bad relationship, your situation will not get better unless you work at it or decide to leave. If you are in debt, you will stay in debt until you make some changes in your spending habits.

Those who complain are often the ones who are refusing to impact their situation. Your choices may be hard, you may face a huge challenge to impact change, and you are not guaranteed success.

However, remaining in the status quo IS guaranteed not to improve your situation.

Taking action is the anecdote to drowning in your current dissatisfaction.

Week 48, Day 4

Get Inspired:

"If life were predictable it would cease to be life and be without flavor."

– Eleanor Roosevelt

Get Aligned:

Chaos can be unsettling. If you are a Type A personality who likes control, order, and predictability, the unknown of chaos can cause stress.

But consider, life is one giant experiment with no guaranteed outcomes! We can do everything right along the way, and still end up sick, poor, alone, or injured. The best we can hope for is to live in alignment with our moral compass, and to embrace as much joy and good fortune as we can along the way.

If you are creating walls and protective barriers around yourself to avoid the unpredictable nature of life, you are indeed missing out on life itself.

Challenge yourself to do something spontaneous this week! It can be alone or with others. But you cannot plan it ahead of time (that would defeat the purpose). Give yourself permission to do something outside of the schedule and see what happens.

Week 48, Day 5

<u>Get Inspired:</u>

"How do you move a mountain, one spoonful of dirt at a time."

-Chinese Proverb

<u>Get Aligned:</u>

When we face a large challenge/problem/shift in life, many of us will default to "paralyze in place" primarily because it's difficult to know where to begin. But begin, you *must*.

Write down the five biggest things you are trying to accomplish in your life right now. Order them from most important to least important.

Begin each day by doing something that impacts the number one item on your list. Catch yourself trying to jump ahead to number four or five (they are often easier to achieve), and resist the urge to work on those projects until you have done that one thing for item number one... Do this Every. Single. Day.

~

A good leader of self has a clear understanding of their big goals and will take daily small actions to support those goals. A good leader to others will replicate the same formula. Ask those who follow you what their number one goal is, then help them to define one tiny task they can do each day to support the pursuit of that goal. Be their cheerleader, accountability partner, and sounding board in this process.

Week 48, Day 6

Get Inspired:

"Move before you are ready."

-unassigned sentiment

Get Aligned:

In life, we must proactively begin before we are truly ready. This bold movement will encourage our spirit, our efforts, and our dedication to rise to the occasion.

This has long been my approach to achieving big far-away goals. I get clear on what it is I want to achieve, I then invest in some general research efforts and planning, and before I am ready or 100% clear on the final product, I announce it to the world. This level of self-applied pressure does wonders for making you reach out of your comfort zone!

As an example:

When I began writing this book it was merely a concept with some basic research. I then publicly announced the book, when I was only a quarter of the way into writing it. After that, I would soon discover just how in-depth and tedious it would be to execute this entire book!

However, I had no choice but to rise to the occasion and give it due focus, because I had already promised a finished version by a tight deadline.

What are you holding back on, that if you made a bold decision or announcement to pursue might take shape faster?

Week 48, Day 7

<u>Reflect:</u>

What inspired you this week?

What will you carry forward?

Week 49, Day 1

Get Inspired:

"Life feels like a game of 'Snakes and Ladders', but without any ladders."

-David Moody

Get Aligned:

There is no easy path in life. It may appear that some are "living the good life" or "have it easy", but that does not exist. Some people do have lucky breaks, but they are not immune to hard times.

Once we accept that no one has left a ladder laying around for us as a handy tool along our personal journey, we can move forward with the business of avoiding the snakes ... or better yet, learning how to tame and navigate the snakes safely.

Don't wait for permission; get to work and actively build the ladders that you need along Your Journey.

Week 49, Day 2

<u>Get Inspired:</u>

"I was taught and raised to never give up, always persevere and no excuses."

-Shaquille O'Neal

<u>Get Aligned:</u>

When something is important to us to achieve, build, or do, it is highly advisable to make this goal public. That may require swallowing your pride or putting your ego on the shelf, but it is much more impactful when working towards your goals. It gives you a public reason to never give up, and to never make excuses.

When I was beginning my business, it was a side hustle. I was still employed full time as a medical sales rep and had just earned my coaching certificate; I was excited to begin building a coaching business. I didn't know exactly how to get those early clients, where to market myself, or the details of how I would grow. I just knew that I had a fire in me that needed air to breathe.

And so, I threw myself a Launch Party. I rented out a friend's art gallery, provided food and drinks, and invited everyone I knew. I mingled with familiar faces … and then I took the stage. I LOVE public speaking, but I was terrified by the talk I was about to give. I was telling my closest friends and family (and a few potential clients) what my plans were for the business, what I could offer them, and why coaching mattered.

What if they thought I was crazy? What if they thought I was a joke? And worse yet, what if the business never actually took off?

There was a lot riding on that moment for my pride and my ego.

Everyone was gracious and encouraging ... and four longggg years later, the business was thriving enough for it to finally become my full-time job.

I knew I had to get on that stage to make it public in a big way. I knew that it would be tough to build a business from scratch (oh, and it was so much tougher than I had even envisioned) and I would be tempted to give it when it got hard. But I also knew that because I had publicly declared what I was building, I would have to find a way to make it happen and not give up on myself.

If you are facing a big dream or project, go ahead and make it public. Use that momentum and pressure to keep yourself accountable to your dream. It may be harder than anticipated with more twists and turns, but it will fuel your fire longer than a private dream behind closed doors.

Commit to action so that you can make forward progress.

Week 49, Day 3

Get Inspired:

"People who have had little self-reflection live life in a huge reality blind-spot."

-Bryant McGill

Get Aligned:

Turning the lens inward when we hit a wall or find ourselves "stuck" can be hard. We have deep seated biases towards ourselves, both positive and negative. This is usually a good time to enlist the help of someone else. Someone without a horse in the race, as they say; someone who can view you objectively without personal judgment. A professional Coach is a great person for this job; they can help you to find your blind spots and to improve your teachability.

Before you rush out to hire a Coach, however, try these exercises at home:

1- Record in a journal how you react to mistakes. Use this information to help guide you as you move to step #2.
2- Challenge yourself to try something new, something that you will likely not be perfect at the first time through. Work to keep your reactions productive when you struggle. As you work on building those positive reactions, move to step #3.
3- Take note of your areas of strength, and double down on learning something new in those areas of your life.

Do you have great people skills, problem solving skills, or technical skills? Focus on expanding your learning in your sweet spot and be sure to focus on your reactions as you grow in those areas.

Tiny actions like these can exponentially fuel our growth over time.

Week 49, Day 4

Get Inspired:

"Dreams don't work unless you take action. The surest way to make your dreams come true is to live them."
— **Roy T. Bennett**

Get Aligned:

I keep a small sign in my office that reads "Dreams Don't Work Unless You Do". Such a simple but powerful reminder of the chain of command.

Yes, we must be the architect of our dreams; realize our vision and believe in our dream. But then we must take ACTION and do something to pursue those dreams. By living as if they were undoubtedly coming true, we accelerate the pace of achieving these dreams.

Do your dreams have to be BIG? Absolutely not. You might dream of saving up $5,000. You might dream of being able to make a presentation without your voice and hands shaking. You might dream of becoming a parent one day. Or you may dream of learning a foreign language.

No matter how big or small your dream is, there is almost no likelihood of it coming true if you take no action. What are you waiting for? Fear is not an excuse; money is not an excuse; time is not an excuse. Start with what is available to you and build on that progress.

~

Owning Your Journey means that you carry the torch of your dream by executing small efforts towards your goals whenever you can.

Week 49, Day 5

Get Inspired:

"All human actions have one or more of these seven causes: chance, nature, compulsion, habit, reason, passion, and desire."
— **Aristotle**

Get Aligned:

When we consider these seven causes of action, it becomes clear that some actions are merely a reaction to emotion or circumstance; while others are thoughtful and planned. In life, we will encounter both types of action. However, when we remain aware of WHY we are acting, we can begin to funnel more of our energy into positive and proactive actions, and less of it into negative or reactive actions.

As you contemplate Owning Your Journey, will you be willing to only react as life unfolds before you? Or will you plan to chart your course and proactively act as you go? There will be plenty of moments on the path when we react to situations that we couldn't foresee; but hopefully we have been training ourselves to react with reason and passion.

Week 49, Day 6

Get Inspired:

"In the end, people should be judged by their actions, since in the end, it was actions that defined everyone."
— **Nicholas Sparks**

Get Aligned:

If a tree falls in the forest, but no one is around to hear it, did it make a noise?

If we have the most purposeful thoughts, and never express them through our actions ... did they even exist?

When our thoughts exist only inside of ourselves, they do not exist to the outside world.

None of us want our eulogy to be a version of "He had great ideas, but for some reason never pulled the trigger on any of them.". We want to be the person who dares to have an idea and/or values, and to live in those concepts. We want to be such strong leaders of ourselves that no one need question who we are. We want to extend kind and supportive energy to others, so that we continue to receive it back in the circle of life. To do any of these things, we must take actions that support our vision. This does not require us to rise up as activists (unless that is your calling); it only requires us to live in accordance with our vision and our values. To practice it daily in our actions.

Week 49, Day 7

Reflect:

What inspired you this week?

What will you carry forward?

Week 50, Day 1

Get Inspired:

"Passion is the log that keeps the fire of purpose blazing."

– Oprah Winfrey

Get Aligned:

When was the last time that you built a wood burning fire? If you have never built one, when was the last time that you were able to sit and bask in the glow of a fire?

If you work with, or watch, a fire long enough … you know that eventually it runs out of energy if left to its own devices; the wood is the source of energy that must be renewed consistently. Someone must continue to stoke and add new logs to the fire if the flames are to continue burning.

When our purpose and our ideas are fresh and bold in our minds, we are full of passion to act. Over time, however, it can be easy for us to run out of energy. We must consistently add logs to our own fire so that we have energy to keep going. Remind yourself WHY you are working so hard towards your dreams.

Are you pushing yourself at work so that you can get that promotion?

Bogged down by fertility challenges as you strive to start a family?

Exhausted by the amount of studying for your higher-level education?

Are you tired of making healthy choices as you work to improve your nutrition?

Tempted to have that drink while trying to stay sober?

Ready to throw in the towel as you get closer to opening your own business?

Stop and remind yourself WHY you started in the first place. Consider a Vision Board or Tracking Calendar to visually keep yourself motivated. Celebrate your progress and little wins along the way. Set smaller targets and goals along the road to the BIG goal. All of this keeps your brain engaged and fuels your passion.

The biggest mistake we can make is getting bogged down in 'doing' and forgetting about the fuel behind the drive.

~

As I sit here typing this page, I am having that same grueling feeling. The process and strain of researching and writing a book is exhausting me. It is time to put a log on the fire. It is serendipitous that I am writing this segment of the book now, and therefore can also remind MYSELF why I am working on this book, why I am taking time away from my family to stare at my computer, what purpose it serves, and who it will benefit.

Reviving your passion may just be the urgent action item needed to support your vision.

Week 50, Day 2

Get Inspired:

"Rituals play very important functions in human societies. They help individuals through their anxieties, connect to one another. They help people find meaning in their lives."

-Dimitris Xygalatas

Get Aligned:

What rituals do you embrace on a daily, weekly, monthly, or yearly basis? Take your time and jot them down in your journal. These should be the bedrock of your life that helps you to feel connected to yourself, and to your community. They help you find shelter when times are chaotic, and energy when you are weak. These may seem small, but they are activities which help us to understand where we are in our day, who we are connected to, and to find a sense of control in the tiny moments of our lives.

Examples of my key rituals include:

-Walking with my dog first thing each morning, while listening to an audible book.

-Doing a quick scan of email checking for time-sensitive challenges early in the morning before the workday begins, but not responding to anything that isn't truly urgent.

-Depositing a kiss and telling my kids "Work hard, do your best, have fun" each day as I drop them at school.

-Closing down my computer and putting my agenda for the next morning on my desk at the end of each workday.

-Saying my gratitude statements as I fall asleep at night.

-Always saying "I love you" to my husband right before I don my eye mask and drift off to sleep.

-Hosting our extended family at our home over Thanksgiving and making space for each person to share what they are thankful for.

-Always joining my family for a 4th of July celebration and fireworks on the water.

-Making my grandma's scratch chocolate cake for birthday celebrations.

~

Rituals are habits with emotion attached to them.

What are your rituals? Consider your personal life, your holiday celebrations, and your work life. Feel free to add new ones as you discover them!

Week 50, Day 3

Get Inspired:

"Don't allow your rituals to become ruts."

-Todd Henry

Get Aligned:

While rituals play a powerful role in helping us to achieve moments of rest and moments of encouragement, they also have a downside.

If we hang onto rituals for "too long" after they are useful to us, they can become ruts that are detrimental to our growth.

If you wish to train for a marathon and have a ritual of running 5 miles each morning … this will likely not prepare you for a true marathon.

If you wish to switch career paths but have a ritual of going to happy hour with colleagues each evening after work, you will likely delay finding the people or opportunities for your next career move.

As a good leader of self, you should examine your rituals from time to time and evaluate how they are helping you in life. If you have outgrown them, make an adjustment.

Week 50, Day 4

Get Inspired:

"Ritual is a terribly important, binding cement in society. If we abandon formality and rituals, we're actually weakening the relationships that exist between people that bind."

-Alexander McCall Smith

Get Aligned:

If cavemen had Instagram, what would it show? Maybe great hunts with successful outcomes; maybe tidy caves with multiple children; possibly big fires and cozy fur cloaks; or plentiful food shared amongst the tribe.

Alas, there was no Instagram (how lucky for them!). Instead, they turned to rituals to stay connected and share stories. Different civilizations did this in their own unique way, but dances, formal attire, feasts, and fire circles were all common means of gathering in ritual.

In modern times, we still rely on rituals to stay connected. Do you post photos on your favorite social media outlet, in hopes of sharing your family story with friends or even to get those photo reminders down the road? Do you ever join friends or colleagues in happy hour or at lunch? Do you go on golf outings or girls' weekends? Each of these are examples of rituals that improve our social connection. If you don't have any social rituals in your life, I challenge you to break out of your comfort zone and invest some time in creating one or two. They will tie you deeper to the people around you and open your eyes to the power of building a supportive tribe. We are not meant to go through this life alone. Solitary confinement is indeed a punishment that hurts the human psyche; do not impose this upon yourself!

As you move forward Owning Your Journey, embrace the trusted people around you to support you, share in the ups and downs with you, and to ground yourself with when times get chaotic.

Week 50, Day 5

Get Inspired:

"What I've learned in research with my colleague Francesca Gino and our other colleagues is that rituals play a number of critical roles: rituals in the face of loss can help us feel less grief, rituals with families can make us feel closer, and rituals with our partners can reinforce our commitment to each other. And by rituals we don't mean "elaborate religious ceremonies" — in our research, we often find that the majority of people's rituals are private and idiosyncratic to them."

-Mike Norton

As quoted in HBR, *The Restorative Power of Ritual* by Scott Berinato, April 02, 2020.

Get Aligned:

Rituals to manage through loss or isolation are supremely important to your mental wellbeing. Rituals are also key activities to maintain personal relationships, or even relationships at work. These do not have to be old family traditions or elaborate activities. Find your own rhythm and be OK with it.

Know the driving force behind your rituals and let that be enough to encourage you forward. If you have children, allow them to help design family rituals over the years. If you are a leader at work, allow your employees to share their ideas for routine ritual gatherings or growth exercises.

Remember, a ritual is an action that serves the purpose of recalling a specific feeling. Lean into it and use it for elevating your spirit or resolve.

Week 50, Day 6

Get Inspired:

"Rituals are the formulas by which harmony is restored."

-Terry Tempest Williams

Get Aligned:

If you wonder what a ritual really is, reflect on this quote.

Rituals should be any activity (big or small) that is restorative or connective in nature. You should feel peace and stillness. Find energy for the day by engaging in your rituals. Some are private to only you, and some involve engaging with others.

Do you hum while you brush your teeth? Do you pray before bed? Do you sit at the table as a family to enjoy meals and share small talk? Do you bring coffee to your co-workers on Fridays?

Each of these are tiny rituals that have the big power to retain that sense of familiar routine which soothes our brains.

~

The process of Owning Your Journey will predispose you to creating productive or comforting rituals along the way. These ritual actions help our brains find a moment of comfort, and we can all use more of that in our lives!

Week 50, Day 7

Reflect:

What inspired you this week?

What will you carry forward?

Week 51, Day 1

Get Inspired:

"Rituals are a good sign to your unconscious that it is time to kick in."

-Anne Lamott

Get Aligned:

Rituals are habits that don't require much thought or effort, yet, if they go unrealized you will feel a gap.

When we settle into a ritual, no matter how small, it frees our brain from the constant stress of examining the situation and making calculated choices of what comes next. Instead, they signal our brain to relax by knowing what comes next. It gives momentary relief to the complex thoughts that rules our executive function, and allows the bliss of autopilot to kick in, even if only momentarily.

Spread throughout the day, rituals give brief but necessary moments of relaxation and recovery to our brains.

Don't be afraid of your rituals (unless, of course, they are unhealthy). See the value in them and work to protect them, just as they work to protect you.

Week 51, Day 2

Get Inspired:

"Often, we are caught in a mental trap of seeing enormously successful people and thinking they are where they are because they have some special gift. Yet a closer look shows that the greatest gift that extraordinarily successful people have over the average person is their ability to get themselves to take action."

— Anthony Robbins

Get Aligned:

Consistency beats natural talent every single time. An enormous amount of research has been done in the world of sports on this very topic, and the results are always the same. He/she who has the determination to keep going, build the skills, and try harder will rise to the top.

Michael Jordan is a classic example. Jordan was not a standout player when he joined the UNC team his freshman year. His coach has shared that he made the team because he had an incredible work ethic. He vowed to make it big, and to do that, he committed to working harder and longer than anyone around him. And I think we all know how well that worked out for Jordan! The official National Basketball Association website states: "By acclamation, Michael Jordan is the greatest basketball player of all time."

You may not aspire to be the greatest athlete in your chosen sport, but if you have goals or desires to be great at anything it is important to remember that the power lies within you. Making a commitment to yourself, your development, and your goals is what it takes to get there.

Don't shy away from success because you think that others got there "overnight" or without a struggle. Social media would have us believe that you can be an instant celebrity with worldly riches; so much of this narrative is manipulated to make us believe in the overnight success story.

In the end, the only sure shot that we can reach our goals (whatever they may be) is to show up and do the work. To try and fail, and to try again.

Week 51, Day 3

Get Inspired:

"Self-discipline is the ability to make yourself do what you should do, when you should do it, whether you feel like it or not."

-Elbert Hubbard

Get Aligned:

We cannot go back and erase the mistakes we have made in the past. It pains me to think of the times where I was not kind, was overly naïve, was too nervous to try, or too stubborn to bend. Looking and longing for the past are wasted efforts; we cannot change the choices already made.

We can, however, learn from them and proceed in a fashion that is more aligned with who we are today. If you have lacked in self-leadership or self-discipline over the years, there is no better day than the present one to get started. As you consider your present and future, don't admonish yourself for not living up to your current standards in the past. Instead, challenge yourself to get started.

You have a finite amount of energy to spend throughout your day. Use it to row the boat forward.

Week 51, Day 4

Get Inspired:

"Vision without action is merely a dream. Action without vision just passes the time. Vision with action can change the world."

-Joel A. Barker

Get Aligned:

Hello goosebumps! This quote NAILS it!

I encourage my clients to build Vision Boards, not Dream Boards. Dreams are lovely thoughts that you never intend to act upon. Visions are burning desires that require action, they are the belly fires that ignite your days, and fill your dreams at night. They hold our attention and demand to be supported.

~

True Story: My personal belly fire was building a business of my own. It consumed me and drove me to action. In the preparatory years and years of side-gigging it I was tired … but the fire was real. During that time the movie "The Greatest Showman" came out, and the song "A Million Dreams" along with it. The message in that song was so intimately related to my desire to build my vision that it became my own personal theme song. It moved me with so much power, it often brought me to tears. Embrace your vision and don't be afraid to feel it. Find your source of energy and encouragement to press through the hard times, because the truth is, some of your big dreams won't be easy to achieve, but they will be worth it.

~

Action for the sake of doing something is no different than scrolling through social media or the TV; it is a time killer. There are moments in life when we absolutely need that mind-numbing action to lull our brains. But don't be fooled into making this the predominant use of your time each day. Action attached to your bold Vision can have profound changes on your life, and the lives of those around you.

As you begin to listen to the Vision that might be buried deep inside of you, plan and execute consistently with Action to support that Vision. Turn the Dream into something tangible.

If the Vision feels too big to Act upon, remember that you can't build a sandcastle without multiple buckets of sand.

What can you start on today? Maybe the low-hanging fruit is research, movement, sleep, a business outline, having a discussion with someone, creating your Vision Board, writing out a calendar plan, or organizing the materials you will need to get going.

Select one action and do it today.

Tomorrow, select another action and do that one thing.

Over time, the sandcastle will begin to reveal itself.

Week 51, Day 5

Get Inspired:

"You are what you do, not what you say you do."

– Carl Jung

Get Aligned:

Our actions speak louder than our words. Becoming a person who lives their values is one of the most admirable quests in life.

You may be an accountant, but who you really are is a loving mom, talented painter, and passionate dancer.

You may be a physician, but who you really are is a curious mind, a positive role model as a baseball coach, passionate about healing others, and a loving spouse.

Don't let your career or your day-to-day role in life box you in. You are more than that. You may have a career that is fueled by passion, or one that is simply a means to pay the bills or provide a lifestyle you crave, and that is ok.

What you choose to do with your time is who you are.

How you speak to and listen to others is who you are.

The way you respond to stress is who you are.

Week 51, Day 6

Get Inspired:

"First, see clearly. Next, act correctly. Finally, endure and accept the world as it is." **-Ryan Holiday**

Get Aligned:

Mr. Holiday has outlined it so simply:

See our path, Act to achieve it, Accept the world as it reacts to or around our personal path.

Simple concept, but difficult in application.

Most of us can see our path if we allow ourselves time to do so. Acting to stay on that path is doable with great habits and a focused approach. But enduring and accepting the external realities can be problematic for many of us.

We can control how we show up, but we cannot control how the world shows up. Therefore, to Own Your Journey requires you to control what you can and accept what you cannot control. We will undoubtedly encounter unforeseen challenges and hostile impacts as we pursue our path. Will you choose to give into these forces or get drawn off course by them? Or will you stay focused on your purposeful path and accept that the journey is not always easy?

Week 51, Day 7

Reflect:

What inspired you this week?

What will you carry forward?

Week 52, Day 1

Get Inspired:

"Our character is basically a composite of our habits. Because they are consistent, often unconscious patterns, they constantly, daily, express our character."

-Stephen Covey

Get Aligned:

If you want to change who you are, you must first change your habits.

What we think, we do. What we do, we are.

Examine who you want to be, how you want to show up, and what character you want to exude. Then clearly assess if your habits are supporting those traits, or if they are impeding them.

If you intend to be a wellness Coach but are making unhealthy decisions by not nurturing or resting your body … it is time for a change.

If you want to be the parent who can pay for their children's college, but you spend any spare money on instant gratification … it is time for a change.

If you want to be a leader at work but find yourself getting caught up in the gossip mill … it is time for a change.

Week 52, Day 2

Get Inspired:

"If we want to change our routine, we don't really need to change the behavior. Rather, we need to find the *cue* that is triggering the nonessential activity or behavior and find a way to associate that same cue with something that *is* essential."

- Greg McKeown, *Essentialism*, Crown Business, 2014, pg. 210.

Get Aligned:

It happens to all of us, we are doing great until suddenly we notice that we have somehow slipped back into nonproductive habits; this is when it's time to shake things up! Look for that trigger to your less-than-desirable-actions and change or replace it with a new one to signal a more productive habit.

Are you trying to do your deep work first thing in the morning, as opposed to getting sucked down the email black hole? Create a signal for yourself, such as sitting at your desk with a cup of coffee and opening only your planner. Resist the old habit of opening email as you sit down.

Breaking old habits is hard, they are deeply engrained. And so, by employing a new smaller and comfortable habit we can slowly but surely create new tracks in our brain that will soon be automatic.

If you go about creating several new habits at once or trying to cut off several old cues at once, you are likely to struggle and possibly fall even farther behind. Instead, start with one small thing. Find a new cue that feels good and ask a friend to help you stay on track by keeping you accountable.

Week 52, Day 3

Get Inspired:

Every action you take is a vote for the type of person you wish to become. No single instance will transform your beliefs, but as the votes build up, so does the evidence of your new identity. This is one reason why meaningful change does not require radical change. Small habits can make a meaningful difference by providing evidence of a new identity. And if a change is meaningful, it is actually big. That's the paradox of making small improvements.

-James Clear

Get Aligned:

If ever there was an authority on micro-habits, it is James Clear.

Sidebar: if you have not read his book, "Atomic Habits", do yourself a favor and order your copy now! It will be time well spent.

In the self-leadership model, executing consistently with thoughtful action is the 4th cornerstone for owning your unique life journey. Once we see the vision, have adjusted our mindset, and show up with authentic presence, we now must take consistent tiny steps of action towards living the life we desire.

If we try to do too much at once, we will surely become exhausted and backslide. If we make tiny adjustments, implement small habits, and align our actions with our vision, we are living as a great leader of self.

Being a great leader of self is not about being perfect. None of us will ever reach that threshold and thank goodness ... it would be so boring! Instead, being a great leader of self is about consistently applying the model to be aware of how we want to show up in life and aligning our thoughts, presence, and actions in tiny ways to that standard whenever possible.

Week 52, Day 4

Get Inspired:

"Whatever you do will be insignificant, but it is very important that you do it."
— **Mahatma Gandhi**

Get Aligned:

Most of us will not be Nobel Prize winners, Celebrities, Olympic athletes, or the President of the United States. The odds are more in favor of us going through life with relative anonymity while pursuing our daily tasks.

Our daily maneuvers may seem insignificant in comparison to these famous positions. Yet, the mundane and routine are important to our individual lives, to our families, to our teams, and to our Own Journey of self-leadership.

Having the commitment to keep showing up in your truth, in pursuing your goals, to put positive energy out into the world around you, and to stay focused on doing the right thing will always be imperative in managing yourself... even if no one ever notices your efforts.

Week 52, Day 5

<u>Get Inspired:</u>

"Action may not always bring happiness, but there is no happiness without action. "
— **William James**

<u>Get Aligned:</u>

Sometimes we will try and fail. That is just how life goes, it is rarely fair.

When we stop making excuses and get down to the business of trying, we are often surprised at how far we get. The act if simply DOING something will bring happiness for our efforts.

If we are too afraid to try, we will certainly stay in limbo. The people who are the "top successes" around you are likely the ones who try more often, try sooner after they fail, and hesitate less before they take action. It is a numbers game; the more you show up and the more swings you take, the more likely you are to get that homerun ... or to at least get on base. You will never feel the rush of a grand slam if you decide to stay on the bench. And who knows, maybe one day you WILL get the grand slam. If not, at least you can have fun trying.

Week 52, Day 6

Get Inspired:

"Follow your bliss and the universe will open doors for you where there were only walls."
— **Joseph Campbell**

Get Aligned:

What is YOUR bliss? Have you ever stopped to acknowledge it?

I am very clear in my bliss, and when I began my own company, it was with that bliss in mind so that I could live in harmony and balance with it. I love working; I love helping people find their own "ah-ha" moments in life; I love helping people to face their challenges and navigate a path forward. I also love being a mom; I love being available to help my kids with the sometimes trite or frustrating tasks that I deem important; I love the excitement of building our intentional life alongside my husband; I love my animals and being connected deeply to Nature every day.

These bliss principles helped me to design how I would work and what I would do for my clients. By acknowledging my bliss, the Universe did (and continues) to open doors that I could never see for myself.

Begin to define your bliss, and let it guide your choices in life. The path WILL rise up to meet you when you embrace this deep level of authenticity.

Begin by writing out your bliss statement or bullet points; what do YOU love? What type of life makes you feel grounded and at peace, while bursting with joy?

~

Being clear in your definition of bliss will help to shape what actions to take and which direction to go when you face cross-roads in life.

Week 52, Day 7

Reflect:

What inspired you this week?

What will you carry forward?

Postscript:

Question- Did you stay the course and learn one day at a time over the past year, or did you devour chunks at a time in accordance with your own internal rhythms?

There is no correct answer! I sincerely hope that you use this book in a way that supports your unique journey, along your own timeline!

I will encourage you to re-read passages that light you up, make you think, or encourage you through a difficult season as often as needed.

~

I know that a vast number of brilliant ideas and concepts exist in the world, and this book brought you a tiny sliver of the pie. Each day was thoughtfully selected to inspire, teach, and encourage you on Your Journey.

I hope throughout this year you have found inspiration as well as practical tips for implementing some new behaviors as you continuously work to Own Your Journey.

Did you notice that quotes or teachings from some individuals were represented more than once? That is for good reason; I encourage you to seek out more wisdom from these great minds, or any of the other leaders included in this text!

~

As a personal result of learning from scholars, thought leaders, scientists, visionaries, students-of-life, and so many others ... I have adopted a belief of how to pursue my Own

Journey: I embrace the knowledge shared with me by *"marrying the woo with the work."*

This simply means that I lean into the facts while also embracing the sometimes "woo-woo" concepts of self-leadership, those less-tangible concepts such as manifestation, abundance, and affirmations. I then bring it all together through my actions and work that I put forward.

~

As a recap, the key elements that I believe bring us each closer to our destiny of Owning Our Journey include the following:

- Know your True North.
- Increase your vibrational energy.
- Steep yourself in gratitude.
- Believe in abundance as you pull away from a space of lack.
- Invest in personal affirmations.
- Manifest your future through your visions and your mindset, allowing your actions to follow.
- Show up authentically to yourself and simultaneously respectfully to others.
- Listen and learn with passion.
- When in doubt, take a step forward.
- You can always pivot if needed.
- Be grounded in your truth.

~

I wish strength and bliss for you as you continue on the path of Owning Your Journey! ~ *Stacy*

Made in the USA
Middletown, DE
06 September 2024